Search and Rescue
K-9

K-9 Name:_____

(It is recommended that each K-9 has its own log book)

Discipline: _____

(It is recommended that each discipline has its own log book)

Dates: _____thru_____

Owner: _____

Address: _____

_____

If found, please return to the Owner listed above.
Standard mailing costs will be reimbursed.

K-9 SAR
Training Log

By Sharolyn L. Sievert

ISBN-13: 978-1514220801
ISBN-10: 1514220806

1. K-9 Training Logs
2. Search and Rescue Operations

Published by: K9 Search Books

www.K9SearchBooks.com

Printed in the United States of America.

Why do we need Training Logs?

Florida v. Harris – SCOTUS 2013:

Requiring the State to introduce comprehensive documentation of the dog's prior hits and misses in the field, and holding that absent field records will preclude a finding of probable cause no matter how much other proof the State offers, is the antithesis of a totality-of-the-circumstances approach. This is made worse by the State Supreme Court's treatment of field-performance records as the evidentiary gold standard when, in fact, such data may not capture a dog's false negatives or may markedly overstate a dog's false positives. Such inaccuracies do not taint records of a dog's performance in <u>standard training and certification settings, making that performance a better measure of a dog's reliability</u>.

Dogs should be trained, certified and reliable.

Training and reliability are determined by Training Logs maintained throughout a dog's career.

Certification verifies the training through third party testing.

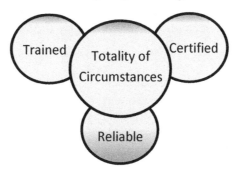

K-9 TRAINING LOG

Unit ☐	Individual ☐	Demo ☐	Meet/Greet ☐

Date: _____ Time of Day: _____ Location: _____

Training Objective: _____

_____

# of Subjects / Hides:	Length/Size of Trail / Area:
Age of Trail/Hide(s):	# Turns/Transitions:
Scent Article: N/A ☐	Is It: Known ☐ Blind ☐ Dbl Blind ☐
Time on Trail / in Area:	Scent Specific? Yes ☐ No ☐ N/A ☐
DoT confirmed? Yes ☐ No ☐ N/A ☐	Field Tech: N/A ☐

Weather: N/A ☐	Temperature: Indoors ☐
Humidity: Low ☐ Medium ☐ High ☐	Wind Speed: Direction:
Environment / Conditions:	

Notes : _____

_____

_____

_____

_____

Reward:	Final Trained Response (FTR):

Mapping: *North* ↑

Were objectives met? Yes ☐ No ☐

Training Officer Review: ☐

K-9 TRAINING LOG

Unit ☐	Individual ☐	Demo ☐	Meet/Greet ☐
Date:	Time of Day:	Location:	

Training Objective:

_____

_____

# of Subjects / Hides:	Length/Size of Trail / Area:
Age of Trail/Hide(s):	# Turns/Transitions:
Scent Article: N/A ☐	Is It: Known ☐ Blind ☐ Dbl Blind ☐
Time on Trail / in Area:	Scent Specific? Yes ☐ No ☐ N/A ☐
DoT confirmed? Yes ☐ No ☐ N/A ☐	Field Tech: N/A ☐

Weather: N/A ☐	Temperature: Indoors ☐
Humidity: Low ☐ Medium ☐ High ☐	Wind Speed: Direction:

Environment / Conditions: _____

Notes :

_____

_____

_____

_____

_____

Reward:	Final Trained Response (FTR):

Mapping: North ⬆

Were objectives met?   Yes ☐   No ☐

Training Officer Review: ☐

K-9 TRAINING LOG

Unit ☐	Individual ☐	Demo ☐	Meet/Greet ☐
Date:	Time of Day:	Location:	

Training Objective:

# of Subjects / Hides:	Length/Size of Trail / Area:
Age of Trail/Hide(s):	# Turns/Transitions:
Scent Article: N/A ☐	Is It: Known ☐ Blind ☐ Dbl Blind ☐
Time on Trail / in Area:	Scent Specific? Yes ☐ No ☐ N/A ☐
DoT confirmed? Yes ☐ No ☐ N/A ☐	Field Tech: N/A ☐

Weather: N/A ☐	Temperature:	Indoors ☐
Humidity: Low ☐ Medium ☐ High ☐	Wind Speed:	Direction:
Environment / Conditions:		

Notes :

Reward:	Final Trained Response (FTR):

Mapping: *North* ↑

Were objectives met? Yes ☐ No ☐

Training Officer Review: ☐

K-9 TRAINING LOG

Unit ☐	Individual ☐	Demo ☐	Meet/Greet ☐
Date:	Time of Day:	Location:	

Training Objective:

# of Subjects / Hides:		Length/Size of Trail / Area:		
Age of Trail/Hide(s):		# Turns/Transitions:		
Scent Article:	N/A ☐	Is It: Known ☐ Blind ☐ Dbl Blind ☐		
Time on Trail / in Area:		Scent Specific? Yes ☐ No ☐	N/A ☐	
DoT confirmed? Yes ☐ No ☐	N/A ☐	Field Tech:	N/A ☐	

Weather:	N/A ☐	Temperature:		Indoors ☐
Humidity: Low ☐ Medium ☐ High ☐		Wind Speed:	Direction:	

Environment / Conditions:

Notes :

Reward:	Final Trained Response (FTR):

Mapping: *North* ⬆

Were objectives met?   Yes ☐ No ☐

Training Officer Review: ☐

K-9 TRAINING LOG

Unit ☐	Individual ☐	Demo ☐	Meet/Greet ☐

Date:	Time of Day:	Location:

Training Objective:

# of Subjects / Hides:	Length/Size of Trail / Area:
Age of Trail/Hide(s):	# Turns/Transitions:
Scent Article: N/A ☐	Is It: Known ☐ Blind ☐ Dbl Blind ☐
Time on Trail / in Area:	Scent Specific? Yes ☐ No ☐ N/A ☐
DoT confirmed? Yes ☐ No ☐ N/A ☐	Field Tech: N/A ☐

Weather: N/A ☐	Temperature: Indoors ☐
Humidity: Low ☐ Medium ☐ High ☐	Wind Speed: Direction:

Environment / Conditions:

Notes :

Reward:	Final Trained Response (FTR):

Mapping: *North* ↑

Were objectives met?   Yes ☐   No ☐

Training Officer Review: ☐

K-9 TRAINING LOG

Unit ☐	Individual ☐	Demo ☐	Meet/Greet ☐
Date:	Time of Day:	Location:	

Training Objective:

# of Subjects / Hides:	Length/Size of Trail / Area:
Age of Trail/Hide(s):	# Turns/Transitions:
Scent Article: N/A ☐	Is It: Known ☐ Blind ☐ Dbl Blind ☐
Time on Trail / in Area:	Scent Specific? Yes ☐ No ☐ N/A ☐
DoT confirmed? Yes ☐ No ☐ N/A ☐	Field Tech: N/A ☐

Weather: N/A ☐	Temperature:	Indoors ☐
Humidity: Low ☐ Medium ☐ High ☐	Wind Speed:	Direction:
Environment / Conditions:		

Notes :

Reward:	*Final Trained Response (FTR):*

Mapping: *North* ⬆

Were objectives met?   Yes ☐   No ☐

Training Officer Review: ☐

K-9 TRAINING LOG

Unit ☐	Individual ☐	Demo ☐	Meet/Greet ☐
Date:	Time of Day:	Location:	

Training Objective:

_____

_____

# of Subjects / Hides:	Length/Size of Trail / Area:
Age of Trail/Hide(s):	# Turns/Transitions:
Scent Article: N/A ☐	Is It: Known ☐ Blind ☐ Dbl Blind ☐
Time on Trail / in Area:	Scent Specific? Yes ☐ No ☐ N/A ☐
DoT confirmed? Yes ☐ No ☐ N/A ☐	Field Tech: N/A ☐
Weather: N/A ☐	Temperature: Indoors ☐
Humidity: Low ☐ Medium ☐ High ☐	Wind Speed:	Direction:

Environment / Conditions:

_____

Notes :

_____

_____

_____

_____

_____

Reward:	*Final Trained Response (FTR):*

Mapping: *North* ↑

Were objectives met?   Yes ☐   No ☐

Training Officer Review: ☐

K-9 TRAINING LOG

Unit ☐	Individual ☐	Demo ☐	Meet/Greet ☐
Date:	Time of Day:	Location:	

Training Objective:

# of Subjects / Hides:	Length/Size of Trail / Area:
Age of Trail/Hide(s):	# Turns/Transitions:
Scent Article: N/A ☐	Is It: Known ☐ Blind ☐ Dbl Blind ☐
Time on Trail / in Area:	Scent Specific? Yes ☐ No ☐ N/A ☐
DoT confirmed? Yes ☐ No ☐ N/A ☐	Field Tech: N/A ☐

Weather: N/A ☐	Temperature: Indoors ☐
Humidity: Low ☐ Medium ☐ High ☐	Wind Speed:	Direction:

Environment / Conditions:

Notes :

Reward:	*Final Trained Response (FTR):*

Mapping: *North* ⬆

Were objectives met?   Yes ☐   No ☐

Training Officer Review: ☐

K-9 TRAINING LOG

Unit ☐	Individual ☐	Demo ☐	Meet/Greet ☐
Date:	Time of Day:	Location:	

Training Objective:

# of Subjects / Hides:	Length/Size of Trail / Area:
Age of Trail/Hide(s):	# Turns/Transitions:
Scent Article: N/A ☐	Is It: Known ☐ Blind ☐ Dbl Blind ☐
Time on Trail / in Area:	Scent Specific? Yes ☐ No ☐ N/A ☐
DoT confirmed? Yes ☐ No ☐ N/A ☐	Field Tech: N/A ☐
Weather: N/A ☐	Temperature: Indoors ☐
Humidity: Low ☐ Medium ☐ High ☐	Wind Speed: Direction:
Environment / Conditions:	

Notes :

Reward:	Final Trained Response (FTR):

Mapping: *North* ↑

Were objectives met? Yes ☐ No ☐

Training Officer Review: ☐

K-9 TRAINING LOG

Unit ☐	Individual ☐	Demo ☐	Meet/Greet ☐
Date:	Time of Day:	Location:	

Training Objective:

_____

_____

# of Subjects / Hides:	Length/Size of Trail / Area:
Age of Trail/Hide(s):	# Turns/Transitions:
Scent Article: N/A ☐	Is It: Known ☐ Blind ☐ Dbl Blind ☐
Time on Trail / in Area:	Scent Specific? Yes ☐ No ☐ N/A ☐
DoT confirmed? Yes ☐ No ☐ N/A ☐	Field Tech: N/A ☐

Weather: N/A ☐	Temperature:	Indoors ☐
Humidity: Low ☐ Medium ☐ High ☐	Wind Speed:	Direction:

Environment / Conditions: _____

Notes : _____

_____

_____

_____

_____

Reward:	*Final Trained Response (FTR):*

Mapping: *North* ↑

Were objectives met?   Yes ☐   No ☐

Training Officer Review: ☐

K-9 TRAINING LOG

Unit ☐	Individual ☐	Demo ☐	Meet/Greet ☐
Date:	Time of Day:	Location:	

Training Objective:

# of Subjects / Hides:		Length/Size of Trail / Area:	
Age of Trail/Hide(s):		# Turns/Transitions:	
Scent Article:	N/A ☐	Is It: Known ☐ Blind ☐ Dbl Blind ☐	
Time on Trail / in Area:		Scent Specific? Yes ☐ No ☐	N/A ☐
DoT confirmed? Yes ☐ No ☐	N/A ☐	Field Tech:	N/A ☐

Weather:	N/A ☐	Temperature:	Indoors ☐
Humidity: Low ☐ Medium ☐ High ☐		Wind Speed:	Direction:

Environment / Conditions:

Notes :

Reward:	Final Trained Response (FTR):

Mapping: *North* ⬆

Were objectives met?   Yes ☐   No ☐

Training Officer Review: ☐

K-9 TRAINING LOG

Unit ☐	Individual ☐	Demo ☐	Meet/Greet ☐
Date:	Time of Day:	Location:	

Training Objective:

# of Subjects / Hides:	Length/Size of Trail / Area:
Age of Trail/Hide(s):	# Turns/Transitions:
Scent Article: N/A ☐	Is It: Known ☐ Blind ☐ Dbl Blind ☐
Time on Trail / in Area:	Scent Specific? Yes ☐ No ☐ N/A ☐
DoT confirmed? Yes ☐ No ☐ N/A ☐	Field Tech: N/A ☐

Weather: N/A ☐	Temperature: Indoors ☐
Humidity: Low ☐ Medium ☐ High ☐	Wind Speed:	Direction:

Environment / Conditions:

Notes :

Reward:	*Final Trained Response (FTR):*

Mapping: *North* ↑

Were objectives met?   Yes ☐ No ☐

Training Officer Review: ☐

K-9 TRAINING LOG

Unit ☐	Individual ☐	Demo ☐	Meet/Greet ☐
Date:	Time of Day:	Location:	

Training Objective:

# of Subjects / Hides:	Length/Size of Trail / Area:
Age of Trail/Hide(s):	# Turns/Transitions:
Scent Article: N/A ☐	Is It: Known ☐ Blind ☐ Dbl Blind ☐
Time on Trail / in Area:	Scent Specific? Yes ☐ No ☐ N/A ☐
DoT confirmed? Yes ☐ No ☐ N/A ☐	Field Tech: N/A ☐
Weather: N/A ☐	Temperature: Indoors ☐
Humidity: Low ☐ Medium ☐ High ☐	Wind Speed: Direction:
Environment / Conditions:	

Notes :

Reward: Final Trained Response (FTR):

Mapping: North ↑

Were objectives met?   Yes ☐   No ☐

Training Officer Review: ☐

K-9 TRAINING LOG

Unit ☐	Individual ☐	Demo ☐	Meet/Greet ☐

Date:	Time of Day:	Location:

Training Objective:

# of Subjects / Hides:	Length/Size of Trail / Area:
Age of Trail/Hide(s):	# Turns/Transitions:
Scent Article: N/A ☐	Is It: Known ☐ Blind ☐ Dbl Blind ☐
Time on Trail / in Area:	Scent Specific? Yes ☐ No ☐ N/A ☐
DoT confirmed? Yes ☐ No ☐ N/A ☐	Field Tech: N/A ☐

Weather: N/A ☐	Temperature: Indoors ☐
Humidity: Low ☐ Medium ☐ High ☐	Wind Speed:	Direction:

Environment / Conditions:

Notes :

Reward:	Final Trained Response (FTR):

Mapping: North ↑

Were objectives met?   Yes ☐   No ☐

Training Officer Review: ☐

K-9 TRAINING LOG

Unit ☐	Individual ☐	Demo ☐	Meet/Greet ☐

Date:	Time of Day:	Location:

Training Objective:

# of Subjects / Hides:	Length/Size of Trail / Area:
Age of Trail/Hide(s):	# Turns/Transitions:
Scent Article: N/A ☐	Is It: Known ☐ Blind ☐ Dbl Blind ☐
Time on Trail / in Area:	Scent Specific? Yes ☐ No ☐ N/A ☐
DoT confirmed? Yes ☐ No ☐ N/A ☐	Field Tech: N/A ☐

Weather: N/A ☐	Temperature: Indoors ☐
Humidity: Low ☐ Medium ☐ High ☐	Wind Speed:	Direction:

Environment / Conditions:

Notes :

Reward:	Final Trained Response (FTR):

Mapping: *North* ↑

Were objectives met?   Yes ☐   No ☐

Training Officer Review: ☐

K-9 TRAINING LOG

Unit ☐	Individual ☐	Demo ☐	Meet/Greet ☐
Date:	Time of Day:	Location:	

Training Objective:

# of Subjects / Hides:	Length/Size of Trail / Area:
Age of Trail/Hide(s):	# Turns/Transitions:
Scent Article: N/A ☐	Is It: Known ☐ Blind ☐ Dbl Blind ☐
Time on Trail / in Area:	Scent Specific? Yes ☐ No ☐ N/A ☐
DoT confirmed? Yes ☐ No ☐ N/A ☐	Field Tech: N/A ☐

Weather: N/A ☐	Temperature: Indoors ☐
Humidity: Low ☐ Medium ☐ High ☐	Wind Speed: Direction:

Environment / Conditions:

Notes :

Reward: | *Final Trained Response (FTR):*

Mapping: *North* ↑

Were objectives met?   Yes ☐   No ☐

Training Officer Review: ☐

K-9 TRAINING LOG

Unit ☐	Individual ☐	Demo ☐	Meet/Greet ☐
Date:	Time of Day:	Location:	

Training Objective:

# of Subjects / Hides:	Length/Size of Trail / Area:
Age of Trail/Hide(s):	# Turns/Transitions:
Scent Article: N/A ☐	Is It: Known ☐ Blind ☐ Dbl Blind ☐
Time on Trail / in Area:	Scent Specific? Yes ☐ No ☐ N/A ☐
DoT confirmed? Yes ☐ No ☐ N/A ☐	Field Tech: N/A ☐

Weather: N/A ☐	Temperature:	Indoors ☐
Humidity: Low ☐ Medium ☐ High ☐	Wind Speed:	Direction:

Environment / Conditions:

Notes :

Reward:	Final Trained Response (FTR):

Mapping: *North* ⬆

Were objectives met?   Yes ☐   No ☐

Training Officer Review: ☐

K-9 TRAINING LOG

Unit ☐	Individual ☐	Demo ☐	Meet/Greet ☐
Date:	Time of Day:	Location:	

Training Objective:

___

# of Subjects / Hides:	Length/Size of Trail / Area:
Age of Trail/Hide(s):	# Turns/Transitions:
Scent Article: N/A ☐	Is It: Known ☐ Blind ☐ Dbl Blind ☐
Time on Trail / in Area:	Scent Specific? Yes ☐ No ☐ N/A ☐
DoT confirmed? Yes ☐ No ☐ N/A ☐	Field Tech: N/A ☐

Weather: N/A ☐	Temperature: Indoors ☐
Humidity: Low ☐ Medium ☐ High ☐	Wind Speed: Direction:
Environment / Conditions:	

Notes :

___

___

___

___

Reward:	Final Trained Response (FTR):

Mapping: *North* ⬆

Were objectives met?   Yes ☐   No ☐

Training Officer Review: ☐

K-9 TRAINING LOG

Unit ☐	Individual ☐	Demo ☐	Meet/Greet ☐
Date:	Time of Day:	Location:	

Training Objective:

# of Subjects / Hides:	Length/Size of Trail / Area:
Age of Trail/Hide(s):	# Turns/Transitions:
Scent Article: N/A ☐	Is It: Known ☐ Blind ☐ Dbl Blind ☐
Time on Trail / in Area:	Scent Specific? Yes ☐ No ☐ N/A ☐
DoT confirmed? Yes ☐ No ☐ N/A ☐	Field Tech: N/A ☐

Weather: N/A ☐	Temperature: Indoors ☐
Humidity: Low ☐ Medium ☐ High ☐	Wind Speed: Direction:
Environment / Conditions:	

Notes :

Reward:	Final Trained Response (FTR):

Mapping: *North* ↑

Were objectives met?   Yes ☐   No ☐

Training Officer Review: ☐

K-9 TRAINING LOG

Unit ☐	Individual ☐	Demo ☐	Meet/Greet ☐

Date:	Time of Day:	Location:

Training Objective:

_____

_____

# of Subjects / Hides:	Length/Size of Trail / Area:
Age of Trail/Hide(s):	# Turns/Transitions:
Scent Article: N/A ☐	Is It: Known ☐ Blind ☐ Dbl Blind ☐
Time on Trail / in Area:	Scent Specific? Yes ☐ No ☐ N/A ☐
DoT confirmed? Yes ☐ No ☐ N/A ☐	Field Tech: N/A ☐

Weather: N/A ☐	Temperature: Indoors ☐
Humidity: Low ☐ Medium ☐ High ☐	Wind Speed:	Direction:

Environment / Conditions:

_____

Notes :

_____

_____

_____

_____

_____

Reward:	*Final Trained Response (FTR):*

Mapping: *North* ⬆

Were objectives met?   Yes ☐   No ☐

Training Officer Review: ☐

K-9 TRAINING LOG

Unit ☐	Individual ☐	Demo ☐	Meet/Greet ☐
Date:	Time of Day:	Location:	

Training Objective:
_____
_____

# of Subjects / Hides:	Length/Size of Trail / Area:
Age of Trail/Hide(s):	# Turns/Transitions:
Scent Article: N/A ☐	Is It: Known ☐ Blind ☐ Dbl Blind ☐
Time on Trail / in Area:	Scent Specific? Yes ☐ No ☐ N/A ☐
DoT confirmed? Yes ☐ No ☐ N/A ☐	Field Tech: N/A ☐

Weather: N/A ☐	Temperature: Indoors ☐
Humidity: Low ☐ Medium ☐ High ☐	Wind Speed:	Direction:

Environment / Conditions:
_____

Notes :
_____
_____
_____
_____
_____

Reward:	Final Trained Response (FTR):

Mapping: North ⬆

Were objectives met?   Yes ☐ No ☐

Training Officer Review: ☐

K-9 TRAINING LOG

Unit ☐	Individual ☐	Demo ☐	Meet/Greet ☐
Date:	Time of Day:	Location:	

Training Objective:

# of Subjects / Hides:	Length/Size of Trail / Area:
Age of Trail/Hide(s):	# Turns/Transitions:
Scent Article: N/A ☐	Is It: Known ☐ Blind ☐ Dbl Blind ☐
Time on Trail / in Area:	Scent Specific? Yes ☐ No ☐ N/A ☐
DoT confirmed? Yes ☐ No ☐ N/A ☐	Field Tech: N/A ☐
Weather: N/A ☐	Temperature: Indoors ☐
Humidity: Low ☐ Medium ☐ High ☐	Wind Speed: Direction:

Environment / Conditions:

Notes :

Reward:	Final Trained Response (FTR):

Mapping: *North* ⬆

Were objectives met?   Yes ☐   No ☐

Training Officer Review: ☐

K-9 TRAINING LOG

Unit ☐	Individual ☐	Demo ☐	Meet/Greet ☐

Date: | Time of Day: | Location:

Training Objective:

_____

_____

# of Subjects / Hides:	Length/Size of Trail / Area:
Age of Trail/Hide(s):	# Turns/Transitions:
Scent Article: N/A ☐	Is It: Known ☐ Blind ☐ Dbl Blind ☐
Time on Trail / in Area:	Scent Specific? Yes ☐ No ☐ N/A ☐
DoT confirmed? Yes ☐ No ☐ N/A ☐	Field Tech: N/A ☐

Weather: N/A ☐	Temperature: Indoors ☐
Humidity: Low ☐ Medium ☐ High ☐	Wind Speed:	Direction:

Environment / Conditions:

_____

Notes :

_____

_____

_____

_____

_____

Reward:	*Final Trained Response (FTR):*

Mapping: *North* ↑

Were objectives met?   Yes ☐   No ☐

Training Officer Review: ☐

K-9 TRAINING LOG

Unit ☐	Individual ☐	Demo ☐	Meet/Greet ☐
Date:	Time of Day:	Location:	

Training Objective:

# of Subjects / Hides:	Length/Size of Trail / Area:
Age of Trail/Hide(s):	# Turns/Transitions:
Scent Article: N/A ☐	Is It: Known ☐ Blind ☐ Dbl Blind ☐
Time on Trail / in Area:	Scent Specific? Yes ☐ No ☐ N/A ☐
DoT confirmed? Yes ☐ No ☐ N/A ☐	Field Tech: N/A ☐

Weather: N/A ☐	Temperature:	Indoors ☐
Humidity: Low ☐ Medium ☐ High ☐	Wind Speed:	Direction:
Environment / Conditions:		

Notes :

Reward:	Final Trained Response (FTR):

Mapping: *North* ↑

Were objectives met?   Yes ☐   No ☐

Training Officer Review: ☐

K-9 TRAINING LOG

Unit ☐	Individual ☐	Demo ☐	Meet/Greet ☐
Date:	Time of Day:	Location:	

Training Objective:

# of Subjects / Hides:	Length/Size of Trail / Area:
Age of Trail/Hide(s):	# Turns/Transitions:
Scent Article: N/A ☐	Is It: Known ☐ Blind ☐ Dbl Blind ☐
Time on Trail / in Area:	Scent Specific? Yes ☐ No ☐ N/A ☐
DoT confirmed? Yes ☐ No ☐ N/A ☐	Field Tech: N/A ☐

Weather: N/A ☐	Temperature:	Indoors ☐
Humidity: Low ☐ Medium ☐ High ☐	Wind Speed:	Direction:
Environment / Conditions:		

Notes :

Reward:	Final Trained Response (FTR):

Mapping: *North* ↑

Were objectives met?   Yes ☐   No ☐

Training Officer Review: ☐

K-9 TRAINING LOG

Unit ☐	Individual ☐	Demo ☐	Meet/Greet ☐
Date:	Time of Day:	Location:	

Training Objective:

# of Subjects / Hides:	Length/Size of Trail / Area:
Age of Trail/Hide(s):	# Turns/Transitions:
Scent Article: N/A ☐	Is It: Known ☐ Blind ☐ Dbl Blind ☐
Time on Trail / in Area:	Scent Specific? Yes ☐ No ☐ N/A ☐
DoT confirmed? Yes ☐ No ☐ N/A ☐	Field Tech: N/A ☐

Weather: N/A ☐	Temperature: Indoors ☐
Humidity: Low ☐ Medium ☐ High ☐	Wind Speed: Direction:

Environment / Conditions:

Notes :

Reward:	Final Trained Response (FTR):

Mapping: _North_ ↑

Were objectives met?   Yes ☐   No ☐

Training Officer Review: ☐

K-9 TRAINING LOG

Unit ☐	Individual ☐	Demo ☐	Meet/Greet ☐

Date: | Time of Day: | Location:

Training Objective:

_____

_____

# of Subjects / Hides:	Length/Size of Trail / Area:
Age of Trail/Hide(s):	# Turns/Transitions:
Scent Article: N/A ☐	Is It: Known ☐ Blind ☐ Dbl Blind ☐
Time on Trail / in Area:	Scent Specific? Yes ☐ No ☐ N/A ☐
DoT confirmed? Yes ☐ No ☐ N/A ☐	Field Tech: N/A ☐
Weather: N/A ☐	Temperature: Indoors ☐
Humidity: Low ☐ Medium ☐ High ☐	Wind Speed:	Direction:
Environment / Conditions:	

Notes :

_____

_____

_____

_____

_____

Reward:	Final Trained Response (FTR):

Mapping: *North* ↑

Were objectives met?   Yes ☐   No ☐

Training Officer Review: ☐

K-9 TRAINING LOG

Unit ☐	Individual ☐	Demo ☐	Meet/Greet ☐
Date:	Time of Day:	Location:	

Training Objective:

# of Subjects / Hides:	Length/Size of Trail / Area:
Age of Trail/Hide(s):	# Turns/Transitions:
Scent Article: N/A ☐	Is It: Known ☐ Blind ☐ Dbl Blind ☐
Time on Trail / in Area:	Scent Specific? Yes ☐ No ☐ N/A ☐
DoT confirmed? Yes ☐ No ☐ N/A ☐	Field Tech: N/A ☐
Weather: N/A ☐	Temperature: Indoors ☐
Humidity: Low ☐ Medium ☐ High ☐	Wind Speed: Direction:

Environment / Conditions:

Notes :

Reward:	Final Trained Response (FTR):

Mapping: *North* ↑

Were objectives met?   Yes ☐   No ☐

Training Officer Review: ☐

K-9 TRAINING LOG

Unit ☐	Individual ☐	Demo ☐	Meet/Greet ☐
Date:	Time of Day:	Location:	

Training Objective:

# of Subjects / Hides:	Length/Size of Trail / Area:
Age of Trail/Hide(s):	# Turns/Transitions:
Scent Article: N/A ☐	Is It: Known ☐ Blind ☐ Dbl Blind ☐
Time on Trail / in Area:	Scent Specific? Yes ☐ No ☐ N/A ☐
DoT confirmed? Yes ☐ No ☐ N/A ☐	Field Tech: N/A ☐

Weather: N/A ☐	Temperature: Indoors ☐
Humidity: Low ☐ Medium ☐ High ☐	Wind Speed: Direction:

Environment / Conditions:

Notes :

Reward:	Final Trained Response (FTR):

Mapping: *North* ↑

Were objectives met? Yes ☐ No ☐

Training Officer Review: ☐

K-9 TRAINING LOG

Unit ☐	Individual ☐	Demo ☐	Meet/Greet ☐
Date:	Time of Day:	Location:	

Training Objective:

# of Subjects / Hides:	Length/Size of Trail / Area:
Age of Trail/Hide(s):	# Turns/Transitions:
Scent Article: N/A ☐	Is It: Known ☐ Blind ☐ Dbl Blind ☐
Time on Trail / in Area:	Scent Specific? Yes ☐ No ☐ N/A ☐
DoT confirmed? Yes ☐ No ☐ N/A ☐	Field Tech: N/A ☐

Weather: N/A ☐	Temperature: Indoors ☐	
Humidity: Low ☐ Medium ☐ High ☐	Wind Speed:	Direction:

Environment / Conditions:

Notes :

Reward:	Final Trained Response (FTR):

Mapping: *North* ⬆

Were objectives met?   Yes ☐   No ☐

Training Officer Review: ☐

K-9 TRAINING LOG

Unit ☐	Individual ☐	Demo ☐	Meet/Greet ☐

Date: _____ | Time of Day: _____ | Location: _____

Training Objective: _____

_____

_____

# of Subjects / Hides:	Length/Size of Trail / Area:
Age of Trail/Hide(s):	# Turns/Transitions:
Scent Article: N/A ☐	Is It: Known ☐ Blind ☐ Dbl Blind ☐
Time on Trail / in Area:	Scent Specific? Yes ☐ No ☐ N/A ☐
DoT confirmed? Yes ☐ No ☐ N/A ☐	Field Tech: N/A ☐
Weather: N/A ☐	Temperature: Indoors ☐
Humidity: Low ☐ Medium ☐ High ☐	Wind Speed: Direction:
Environment / Conditions:	

Notes : _____

_____

_____

_____

_____

_____

Reward:	Final Trained Response (FTR):

Mapping: *North* ↑

Were objectives met?   Yes ☐   No ☐

Training Officer Review: ☐

K-9 TRAINING LOG

Unit ☐	Individual ☐	Demo ☐	Meet/Greet ☐

Date:	Time of Day:	Location:

Training Objective:

_____

_____

# of Subjects / Hides:	Length/Size of Trail / Area:
Age of Trail/Hide(s):	# Turns/Transitions:
Scent Article: N/A ☐	Is It: Known ☐ Blind ☐ Dbl Blind ☐
Time on Trail / in Area:	Scent Specific? Yes ☐ No ☐ N/A ☐
DoT confirmed? Yes ☐ No ☐ N/A ☐	Field Tech: N/A ☐

Weather: N/A ☐	Temperature: Indoors ☐
Humidity: Low ☐ Medium ☐ High ☐	Wind Speed: Direction:

Environment / Conditions: _____

_____

Notes : _____

_____

_____

_____

_____

Reward:	*Final Trained Response (FTR):*

Mapping: *North* ↑

Were objectives met?   Yes ☐   No ☐

Training Officer Review: ☐

K-9 TRAINING LOG

Unit ☐	Individual ☐	Demo ☐	Meet/Greet ☐

Date:	Time of Day:	Location:

Training Objective:

_____

_____

# of Subjects / Hides:	Length/Size of Trail / Area:
Age of Trail/Hide(s):	# Turns/Transitions:
Scent Article: N/A ☐	Is It: Known ☐ Blind ☐ Dbl Blind ☐
Time on Trail / in Area:	Scent Specific? Yes ☐ No ☐ N/A ☐
DoT confirmed? Yes ☐ No ☐ N/A ☐	Field Tech: N/A ☐

Weather: N/A ☐	Temperature: Indoors ☐
Humidity: Low ☐ Medium ☐ High ☐	Wind Speed: Direction:

Environment / Conditions: _____

Notes : _____

_____

_____

_____

_____

Reward:	Final Trained Response (FTR):

Mapping: North ↑

Were objectives met?   Yes ☐   No ☐

Training Officer Review: ☐

K-9 TRAINING LOG

Unit ☐	Individual ☐	Demo ☐	Meet/Greet ☐
Date:	Time of Day:	Location:	

Training Objective:

# of Subjects / Hides:		Length/Size of Trail / Area:	
Age of Trail/Hide(s):		# Turns/Transitions:	
Scent Article:	N/A ☐	Is It: Known ☐ Blind ☐ Dbl Blind ☐	
Time on Trail / in Area:		Scent Specific? Yes ☐ No ☐	N/A ☐
DoT confirmed? Yes ☐ No ☐	N/A ☐	Field Tech:	N/A ☐
Weather:	N/A ☐	Temperature:	Indoors ☐
Humidity: Low ☐ Medium ☐ High ☐		Wind Speed:	Direction:

Environment / Conditions:

Notes :

Reward:	Final Trained Response (FTR):

Mapping: *North* ↑

Were objectives met?   Yes ☐   No ☐

Training Officer Review: ☐

K-9 TRAINING LOG

Unit ☐	Individual ☐	Demo ☐	Meet/Greet ☐
Date:	Time of Day:	Location:	

Training Objective:

_____

_____

# of Subjects / Hides:		Length/Size of Trail / Area:	
Age of Trail/Hide(s):		# Turns/Transitions:	
Scent Article:	N/A ☐	Is It: Known ☐ Blind ☐ Dbl Blind ☐	
Time on Trail / in Area:		Scent Specific? Yes ☐ No ☐	N/A ☐
DoT confirmed? Yes ☐ No ☐	N/A ☐	Field Tech:	N/A ☐
Weather:	N/A ☐	Temperature:	Indoors ☐
Humidity: Low ☐ Medium ☐ High ☐		Wind Speed:	Direction:
Environment / Conditions:			

Notes :

_____

_____

_____

_____

_____

Reward:	Final Trained Response (FTR):

Mapping: North ⬆

[grid]

Were objectives met?   Yes ☐   No ☐

Training Officer Review: ☐

K-9 TRAINING LOG

Unit ☐	Individual ☐	Demo ☐	Meet/Greet ☐
Date:	Time of Day:	Location:	

Training Objective:

# of Subjects / Hides:	Length/Size of Trail / Area:
Age of Trail/Hide(s):	# Turns/Transitions:
Scent Article: N/A ☐	Is It: Known ☐ Blind ☐ Dbl Blind ☐
Time on Trail / in Area:	Scent Specific? Yes ☐ No ☐ N/A ☐
DoT confirmed? Yes ☐ No ☐ N/A ☐	Field Tech: N/A ☐

Weather: N/A ☐	Temperature: Indoors ☐
Humidity: Low ☐ Medium ☐ High ☐	Wind Speed:	Direction:

Environment / Conditions:

Notes :

Reward:	Final Trained Response (FTR):

Mapping: *North* ⬆

Were objectives met?   Yes ☐   No ☐

Training Officer Review: ☐

K-9 TRAINING LOG

Unit ☐	Individual ☐	Demo ☐	Meet/Greet ☐
Date:	Time of Day:	Location:	

Training Objective:

# of Subjects / Hides:	Length/Size of Trail / Area:
Age of Trail/Hide(s):	# Turns/Transitions:
Scent Article: N/A ☐	Is It: Known ☐ Blind ☐ Dbl Blind ☐
Time on Trail / in Area:	Scent Specific? Yes ☐ No ☐ N/A ☐
DoT confirmed? Yes ☐ No ☐ N/A ☐	Field Tech: N/A ☐

Weather: N/A ☐	Temperature: Indoors ☐
Humidity: Low ☐ Medium ☐ High ☐	Wind Speed:	Direction:

Environment / Conditions:

Notes :

Reward:	Final Trained Response (FTR):

Mapping: *North* ↑

Were objectives met?   Yes ☐ No ☐

Training Officer Review: ☐

K-9 TRAINING LOG

Unit ☐	Individual ☐	Demo ☐	Meet/Greet ☐
Date:	Time of Day:	Location:	

Training Objective:

# of Subjects / Hides:	Length/Size of Trail / Area:
Age of Trail/Hide(s):	# Turns/Transitions:
Scent Article: N/A ☐	Is It: Known ☐ Blind ☐ Dbl Blind ☐
Time on Trail / in Area:	Scent Specific? Yes ☐ No ☐ N/A ☐
DoT confirmed? Yes ☐ No ☐ N/A ☐	Field Tech: N/A ☐

Weather: N/A ☐	Temperature: Indoors ☐
Humidity: Low ☐ Medium ☐ High ☐	Wind Speed:	Direction:
Environment / Conditions:	

Notes :

Reward:	Final Trained Response (FTR):

Mapping: North ↑

Were objectives met?   Yes ☐   No ☐

Training Officer Review: ☐

K-9 TRAINING LOG

Unit ☐	Individual ☐	Demo ☐	Meet/Greet ☐
Date:	Time of Day:	Location:	

Training Objective:

_____

_____

# of Subjects / Hides:	Length/Size of Trail / Area:
Age of Trail/Hide(s):	# Turns/Transitions:
Scent Article: N/A ☐	Is It: Known ☐ Blind ☐ Dbl Blind ☐
Time on Trail / in Area:	Scent Specific? Yes ☐ No ☐ N/A ☐
DoT confirmed? Yes ☐ No ☐ N/A ☐	Field Tech: N/A ☐

Weather: N/A ☐	Temperature: Indoors ☐
Humidity: Low ☐ Medium ☐ High ☐	Wind Speed:	Direction:

Environment / Conditions:

_____

Notes :

_____

_____

_____

_____

Reward:	Final Trained Response (FTR):

Mapping: North ↑

Were objectives met?   Yes ☐   No ☐

Training Officer Review: ☐

K-9 TRAINING LOG

Unit ☐	Individual ☐	Demo ☐	Meet/Greet ☐

Date:	Time of Day:	Location:

Training Objective:

_____

_____

# of Subjects / Hides:	Length/Size of Trail / Area:
Age of Trail/Hide(s):	# Turns/Transitions:
Scent Article: N/A ☐	Is It: Known ☐ Blind ☐ Dbl Blind ☐
Time on Trail / in Area:	Scent Specific? Yes ☐ No ☐ N/A ☐
DoT confirmed? Yes ☐ No ☐ N/A ☐	Field Tech: N/A ☐

Weather: N/A ☐	Temperature: Indoors ☐
Humidity: Low ☐ Medium ☐ High ☐	Wind Speed:	Direction:

Environment / Conditions: _____

Notes :

_____

_____

_____

_____

_____

Reward:	_Final Trained Response (FTR):_

Mapping: _North_ ⬆

Were objectives met?   Yes ☐   No ☐

Training Officer Review: ☐

K-9 TRAINING LOG

Unit ☐	Individual ☐	Demo ☐	Meet/Greet ☐
Date:	Time of Day:	Location:	

Training Objective:

# of Subjects / Hides:	Length/Size of Trail / Area:
Age of Trail/Hide(s):	# Turns/Transitions:
Scent Article: N/A ☐	Is It: Known ☐ Blind ☐ Dbl Blind ☐
Time on Trail / in Area:	Scent Specific? Yes ☐ No ☐ N/A ☐
DoT confirmed? Yes ☐ No ☐ N/A ☐	Field Tech: N/A ☐

Weather: N/A ☐	Temperature: Indoors ☐
Humidity: Low ☐ Medium ☐ High ☐	Wind Speed:	Direction:
Environment / Conditions:	

Notes :

Reward:	Final Trained Response (FTR):

Mapping: North ↑

Were objectives met?   Yes ☐   No ☐

Training Officer Review: ☐

K-9 TRAINING LOG

Unit ☐	Individual ☐	Demo ☐	Meet/Greet ☐

Date: | Time of Day: | Location:

Training Objective: _____

_____

_____

# of Subjects / Hides:	Length/Size of Trail / Area:
Age of Trail/Hide(s):	# Turns/Transitions:
Scent Article: N/A ☐	Is It: Known ☐ Blind ☐ Dbl Blind ☐
Time on Trail / in Area:	Scent Specific? Yes ☐ No ☐ N/A ☐
DoT confirmed? Yes ☐ No ☐ N/A ☐	Field Tech: N/A ☐

Weather: N/A ☐	Temperature: Indoors ☐
Humidity: Low ☐ Medium ☐ High ☐	Wind Speed:	Direction:

Environment / Conditions: _____

Notes : _____

_____

_____

_____

_____

Reward:	*Final Trained Response (FTR):*

Mapping: *North* ↑

Were objectives met?   Yes ☐   No ☐

Training Officer Review: ☐

K-9 TRAINING LOG

Unit ☐	Individual ☐	Demo ☐	Meet/Greet ☐
Date:	Time of Day:	Location:	

Training Objective:
_____
_____

# of Subjects / Hides:	Length/Size of Trail / Area:
Age of Trail/Hide(s):	# Turns/Transitions:
Scent Article: N/A ☐	Is It: Known ☐ Blind ☐ Dbl Blind ☐
Time on Trail / in Area:	Scent Specific? Yes ☐ No ☐ N/A ☐
DoT confirmed? Yes ☐ No ☐ N/A ☐	Field Tech: N/A ☐

Weather: N/A ☐	Temperature: Indoors ☐
Humidity: Low ☐ Medium ☐ High ☐	Wind Speed: Direction:

Environment / Conditions:
_____

Notes :
_____
_____
_____
_____
_____

Reward:	*Final Trained Response (FTR):*

Mapping: *North* ↑

Were objectives met? Yes ☐ No ☐

Training Officer Review: ☐

K-9 TRAINING LOG

Unit ☐	Individual ☐	Demo ☐	Meet/Greet ☐

Date:	Time of Day:	Location:

Training Objective:

# of Subjects / Hides:	Length/Size of Trail / Area:
Age of Trail/Hide(s):	# Turns/Transitions:
Scent Article: N/A ☐	Is It: Known ☐ Blind ☐ Dbl Blind ☐
Time on Trail / in Area:	Scent Specific? Yes ☐ No ☐ N/A ☐
DoT confirmed? Yes ☐ No ☐ N/A ☐	Field Tech: N/A ☐

Weather: N/A ☐	Temperature: Indoors ☐
Humidity: Low ☐ Medium ☐ High ☐	Wind Speed:	Direction:

Environment / Conditions:

Notes :

Reward:	Final Trained Response (FTR):

Mapping: North ⬆

Were objectives met?   Yes ☐   No ☐

Training Officer Review: ☐

K-9 TRAINING LOG

Unit ☐	Individual ☐	Demo ☐	Meet/Greet ☐

Date:	Time of Day:	Location:

Training Objective:

_____

_____

# of Subjects / Hides:		Length/Size of Trail / Area:	
Age of Trail/Hide(s):		# Turns/Transitions:	
Scent Article:	N/A ☐	Is It: Known ☐ Blind ☐ Dbl Blind ☐	
Time on Trail / in Area:		Scent Specific? Yes ☐ No ☐	N/A ☐
DoT confirmed? Yes ☐ No ☐ N/A ☐		Field Tech:	N/A ☐
Weather:	N/A ☐	Temperature:	Indoors ☐
Humidity: Low ☐ Medium ☐ High ☐		Wind Speed:	Direction:
Environment / Conditions:			

Notes :

_____

_____

_____

_____

_____

Reward:	_Final Trained Response (FTR):_

Mapping: _North_ ↑

Were objectives met?   Yes ☐   No ☐

Training Officer Review: ☐

K-9 TRAINING LOG

Unit ☐	Individual ☐	Demo ☐	Meet/Greet ☐
Date:	Time of Day:	Location:	

Training Objective:

# of Subjects / Hides:	Length/Size of Trail / Area:
Age of Trail/Hide(s):	# Turns/Transitions:
Scent Article: N/A ☐	Is It: Known ☐ Blind ☐ Dbl Blind ☐
Time on Trail / in Area:	Scent Specific? Yes ☐ No ☐ N/A ☐
DoT confirmed? Yes ☐ No ☐ N/A ☐	Field Tech: N/A ☐

Weather: N/A ☐	Temperature: Indoors ☐
Humidity: Low ☐ Medium ☐ High ☐	Wind Speed:	Direction:

Environment / Conditions:

Notes :

Reward:	Final Trained Response (FTR):

Mapping: *North* ⬆

Were objectives met?   Yes ☐   No ☐

Training Officer Review: ☐

K-9 TRAINING LOG

Unit ☐	Individual ☐	Demo ☐	Meet/Greet ☐

Date:	Time of Day:	Location:

Training Objective:

_____

_____

# of Subjects / Hides:	Length/Size of Trail / Area:
Age of Trail/Hide(s):	# Turns/Transitions:
Scent Article: N/A ☐	Is It: Known ☐ Blind ☐ Dbl Blind ☐
Time on Trail / in Area:	Scent Specific? Yes ☐ No ☐ N/A ☐
DoT confirmed? Yes ☐ No ☐ N/A ☐	Field Tech: N/A ☐

Weather: N/A ☐	Temperature: Indoors ☐
Humidity: Low ☐ Medium ☐ High ☐	Wind Speed:	Direction:

Environment / Conditions:

_____

Notes :

_____

_____

_____

_____

_____

Reward:	Final Trained Response (FTR):

Mapping: *North* ↟

Were objectives met?   Yes ☐   No ☐

Training Officer Review: ☐

K-9 TRAINING LOG

Unit ☐	Individual ☐	Demo ☐	Meet/Greet ☐
Date:	Time of Day:	Location:	

Training Objective:

# of Subjects / Hides:	Length/Size of Trail / Area:
Age of Trail/Hide(s):	# Turns/Transitions:
Scent Article: N/A ☐	Is It: Known ☐ Blind ☐ Dbl Blind ☐
Time on Trail / in Area:	Scent Specific? Yes ☐ No ☐ N/A ☐
DoT confirmed? Yes ☐ No ☐ N/A ☐	Field Tech: N/A ☐

Weather: N/A ☐	Temperature: Indoors ☐
Humidity: Low ☐ Medium ☐ High ☐	Wind Speed: | Direction:

Environment / Conditions:

Notes :

Reward:	Final Trained Response (FTR):

Mapping: *North* ↑

Were objectives met?   Yes ☐   No ☐

Training Officer Review: ☐

K-9 TRAINING LOG

Unit ☐	Individual ☐	Demo ☐	Meet/Greet ☐
Date:	Time of Day:	Location:	

Training Objective:

# of Subjects / Hides:	Length/Size of Trail / Area:
Age of Trail/Hide(s):	# Turns/Transitions:
Scent Article: N/A ☐	Is It: Known ☐ Blind ☐ Dbl Blind ☐
Time on Trail / in Area:	Scent Specific? Yes ☐ No ☐ N/A ☐
DoT confirmed? Yes ☐ No ☐ N/A ☐	Field Tech: N/A ☐

Weather: N/A ☐	Temperature: Indoors ☐
Humidity: Low ☐ Medium ☐ High ☐	Wind Speed:	Direction:

Environment / Conditions:

Notes :

Reward:	Final Trained Response (FTR):

Mapping: *North* ↑

Were objectives met? Yes ☐ No ☐

Training Officer Review: ☐

K-9 TRAINING LOG

Unit ☐	Individual ☐	Demo ☐	Meet/Greet ☐

Date:	Time of Day:	Location:

Training Objective:

_____

_____

# of Subjects / Hides:	Length/Size of Trail / Area:
Age of Trail/Hide(s):	# Turns/Transitions:
Scent Article: N/A ☐	Is It: Known ☐ Blind ☐ Dbl Blind ☐
Time on Trail / in Area:	Scent Specific? Yes ☐ No ☐ N/A ☐
DoT confirmed? Yes ☐ No ☐ N/A ☐	Field Tech: N/A ☐

Weather: N/A ☐	Temperature: Indoors ☐	
Humidity: Low ☐ Medium ☐ High ☐	Wind Speed:	Direction:

Environment / Conditions: _____

Notes : _____

_____

_____

_____

_____

Reward:	*Final Trained Response (FTR):*

Mapping: *North* ↑

Were objectives met?   Yes ☐   No ☐

Training Officer Review: ☐

K-9 TRAINING LOG

Unit ☐	Individual ☐	Demo ☐	Meet/Greet ☐
Date:	Time of Day:	Location:	

Training Objective:

# of Subjects / Hides:	Length/Size of Trail / Area:
Age of Trail/Hide(s):	# Turns/Transitions:
Scent Article: N/A ☐	Is It: Known ☐ Blind ☐ Dbl Blind ☐
Time on Trail / in Area:	Scent Specific? Yes ☐ No ☐ N/A ☐
DoT confirmed? Yes ☐ No ☐ N/A ☐	Field Tech: N/A ☐

Weather: N/A ☐	Temperature: Indoors ☐
Humidity: Low ☐ Medium ☐ High ☐	Wind Speed:	Direction:

Environment / Conditions:

Notes :

Reward:	Final Trained Response (FTR):

Mapping: North ⬆

Were objectives met?   Yes ☐   No ☐

Training Officer Review: ☐

K-9 TRAINING LOG

Unit ☐	Individual ☐	Demo ☐	Meet/Greet ☐
Date:	Time of Day:	Location:	

Training Objective:

# of Subjects / Hides:	Length/Size of Trail / Area:
Age of Trail/Hide(s):	# Turns/Transitions:
Scent Article: N/A ☐	Is It: Known ☐ Blind ☐ Dbl Blind ☐
Time on Trail / in Area:	Scent Specific? Yes ☐ No ☐ N/A ☐
DoT confirmed? Yes ☐ No ☐ N/A ☐	Field Tech: N/A ☐

Weather: N/A ☐	Temperature: Indoors ☐
Humidity: Low ☐ Medium ☐ High ☐	Wind Speed: Direction:

Environment / Conditions:

Notes :

Reward:	Final Trained Response (FTR):

Mapping: *North* ↑

Were objectives met?   Yes ☐   No ☐

Training Officer Review: ☐

K-9 TRAINING LOG

Unit ☐	Individual ☐	Demo ☐	Meet/Greet ☐
Date:	Time of Day:	Location:	

Training Objective:

# of Subjects / Hides:	Length/Size of Trail / Area:
Age of Trail/Hide(s):	# Turns/Transitions:
Scent Article:　　　　　　　　N/A ☐	Is It: Known ☐　Blind ☐　Dbl Blind ☐
Time on Trail / in Area:	Scent Specific? Yes ☐ No ☐　　N/A ☐
DoT confirmed? Yes ☐ No ☐　　N/A ☐	Field Tech:　　　　　　　　　N/A ☐

Weather:　　　　　　　　　　N/A ☐	Temperature:　　　　　Indoors ☐
Humidity: Low ☐ Medium ☐ High ☐	Wind Speed:　　　　Direction:
Environment / Conditions:	

Notes :

Reward:	Final Trained Response (FTR):

Mapping:　　　　　　　　　　　　　　　　　　　　　　North ⬆

Were objectives met?　　Yes ☐　No ☐

Training Officer Review:　☐

K-9 TRAINING LOG

Unit ☐	Individual ☐	Demo ☐	Meet/Greet ☐

Date:	Time of Day:	Location:

Training Objective: _____

_____

_____

# of Subjects / Hides:	Length/Size of Trail / Area:
Age of Trail/Hide(s):	# Turns/Transitions:
Scent Article: N/A ☐	Is It: Known ☐ Blind ☐ Dbl Blind ☐
Time on Trail / in Area:	Scent Specific? Yes ☐ No ☐ N/A ☐
DoT confirmed? Yes ☐ No ☐ N/A ☐	Field Tech: N/A ☐

Weather: N/A ☐	Temperature: Indoors ☐
Humidity: Low ☐ Medium ☐ High ☐	Wind Speed:	Direction:

Environment / Conditions: _____

Notes : _____

_____

_____

_____

Reward:	Final Trained Response (FTR):

Mapping: *North* ⬆

Were objectives met?   Yes ☐   No ☐

Training Officer Review: ☐

K-9 TRAINING LOG

Unit ☐	Individual ☐	Demo ☐	Meet/Greet ☐
Date:	Time of Day:	Location:	

Training Objective:

_____

_____

# of Subjects / Hides:	Length/Size of Trail / Area:
Age of Trail/Hide(s):	# Turns/Transitions:
Scent Article: N/A ☐	Is It: Known ☐ Blind ☐ Dbl Blind ☐
Time on Trail / in Area:	Scent Specific? Yes ☐ No ☐ N/A ☐
DoT confirmed? Yes ☐ No ☐ N/A ☐	Field Tech: N/A ☐
Weather: N/A ☐	Temperature: Indoors ☐
Humidity: Low ☐ Medium ☐ High ☐	Wind Speed:	Direction:
Environment / Conditions:	

Notes :

_____

_____

_____

_____

_____

Reward:	Final Trained Response (FTR):

Mapping: *North* ↑

Were objectives met?   Yes ☐   No ☐

Training Officer Review: ☐

K-9 TRAINING LOG

Unit ☐	Individual ☐	Demo ☐	Meet/Greet ☐

Date:	Time of Day:	Location:

Training Objective:

# of Subjects / Hides:	Length/Size of Trail / Area:
Age of Trail/Hide(s):	# Turns/Transitions:
Scent Article: N/A ☐	Is It: Known ☐ Blind ☐ Dbl Blind ☐
Time on Trail / in Area:	Scent Specific? Yes ☐ No ☐ N/A ☐
DoT confirmed? Yes ☐ No ☐ N/A ☐	Field Tech: N/A ☐

Weather: N/A ☐	Temperature: Indoors ☐
Humidity: Low ☐ Medium ☐ High ☐	Wind Speed:	Direction:

Environment / Conditions:

Notes :

Reward:	Final Trained Response (FTR):

Mapping: *North* ↑

Were objectives met?   Yes ☐   No ☐

Training Officer Review: ☐

K-9 TRAINING LOG

Unit ☐	Individual ☐	Demo ☐	Meet/Greet ☐

Date:	Time of Day:	Location:

Training Objective:

_____

_____

# of Subjects / Hides:	Length/Size of Trail / Area:
Age of Trail/Hide(s):	# Turns/Transitions:
Scent Article: N/A ☐	Is It: Known ☐ Blind ☐ Dbl Blind ☐
Time on Trail / in Area:	Scent Specific? Yes ☐ No ☐ N/A ☐
DoT confirmed? Yes ☐ No ☐ N/A ☐	Field Tech: N/A ☐

Weather: N/A ☐	Temperature: Indoors ☐
Humidity: Low ☐ Medium ☐ High ☐	Wind Speed:	Direction:

Environment / Conditions:

_____

Notes :

_____

_____

_____

_____

_____

Reward:	Final Trained Response (FTR):

Mapping: *North* ↑

Were objectives met?   Yes ☐   No ☐

Training Officer Review: ☐

K-9 TRAINING LOG

Unit ☐	Individual ☐	Demo ☐	Meet/Greet ☐
Date:	Time of Day:	Location:	

Training Objective:

# of Subjects / Hides:		Length/Size of Trail / Area:		
Age of Trail/Hide(s):		# Turns/Transitions:		
Scent Article:	N/A ☐	Is It: Known ☐ Blind ☐ Dbl Blind ☐		
Time on Trail / in Area:		Scent Specific? Yes ☐ No ☐	N/A ☐	
DoT confirmed? Yes ☐ No ☐	N/A ☐	Field Tech:	N/A ☐	

Weather:	N/A ☐	Temperature:	Indoors ☐
Humidity: Low ☐ Medium ☐ High ☐	Wind Speed:	Direction:	

Environment / Conditions:

Notes :

Reward:	*Final Trained Response (FTR):*

Mapping: *North* ↑

Were objectives met?   Yes ☐   No ☐

Training Officer Review: ☐

K-9 TRAINING LOG

Unit ☐	Individual ☐	Demo ☐	Meet/Greet ☐

Date:	Time of Day:	Location:

Training Objective:

# of Subjects / Hides:	Length/Size of Trail / Area:
Age of Trail/Hide(s):	# Turns/Transitions:
Scent Article: N/A ☐	Is It: Known ☐ Blind ☐ Dbl Blind ☐
Time on Trail / in Area:	Scent Specific? Yes ☐ No ☐ N/A ☐
DoT confirmed? Yes ☐ No ☐ N/A ☐	Field Tech: N/A ☐

Weather: N/A ☐	Temperature: Indoors ☐
Humidity: Low ☐ Medium ☐ High ☐	Wind Speed:	Direction:

Environment / Conditions:

Notes :

Reward:	Final Trained Response (FTR):

Mapping: *North* ↑

Were objectives met?   Yes ☐   No ☐

Training Officer Review: ☐

K-9 TRAINING LOG

Unit ☐	Individual ☐	Demo ☐	Meet/Greet ☐

Date:	Time of Day:	Location:

Training Objective:

# of Subjects / Hides:	Length/Size of Trail / Area:
Age of Trail/Hide(s):	# Turns/Transitions:
Scent Article: N/A ☐	Is It: Known ☐ Blind ☐ Dbl Blind ☐
Time on Trail / in Area:	Scent Specific? Yes ☐ No ☐ N/A ☐
DoT confirmed? Yes ☐ No ☐ N/A ☐	Field Tech: N/A ☐

Weather: N/A ☐	Temperature: Indoors ☐
Humidity: Low ☐ Medium ☐ High ☐	Wind Speed:	Direction:

Environment / Conditions:

Notes :

Reward:	Final Trained Response (FTR):

Mapping: *North* ↑

Were objectives met?   Yes ☐   No ☐

Training Officer Review: ☐

K-9 TRAINING LOG

Unit ☐	Individual ☐	Demo ☐	Meet/Greet ☐
Date:	Time of Day:	Location:	

Training Objective:
_____

_____

# of Subjects / Hides:	Length/Size of Trail / Area:
Age of Trail/Hide(s):	# Turns/Transitions:
Scent Article: N/A ☐	Is It: Known ☐ Blind ☐ Dbl Blind ☐
Time on Trail / in Area:	Scent Specific? Yes ☐ No ☐ N/A ☐
DoT confirmed? Yes ☐ No ☐ N/A ☐	Field Tech: N/A ☐

Weather: N/A ☐	Temperature: Indoors ☐
Humidity: Low ☐ Medium ☐ High ☐	Wind Speed:	Direction:

Environment / Conditions:
_____

Notes :
_____

_____

_____

_____

_____

Reward:	*Final Trained Response (FTR):*

Mapping: *North* ⬆

Were objectives met?   Yes ☐ No ☐

Training Officer Review: ☐

K-9 TRAINING LOG

Unit ☐	Individual ☐	Demo ☐	Meet/Greet ☐

Date:	Time of Day:	Location:

Training Objective:

# of Subjects / Hides:	Length/Size of Trail / Area:
Age of Trail/Hide(s):	# Turns/Transitions:
Scent Article: N/A ☐	Is It: Known ☐ Blind ☐ Dbl Blind ☐
Time on Trail / in Area:	Scent Specific? Yes ☐ No ☐ N/A ☐
DoT confirmed? Yes ☐ No ☐ N/A ☐	Field Tech: N/A ☐

Weather: N/A ☐	Temperature: Indoors ☐
Humidity: Low ☐ Medium ☐ High ☐	Wind Speed:	Direction:

Environment / Conditions:

Notes :

Reward:	Final Trained Response (FTR):

Mapping: North ↑

Were objectives met?   Yes ☐   No ☐

Training Officer Review: ☐

K-9 TRAINING LOG

Unit ☐	Individual ☐	Demo ☐	Meet/Greet ☐
Date:	Time of Day:	Location:	

Training Objective:

# of Subjects / Hides:	Length/Size of Trail / Area:
Age of Trail/Hide(s):	# Turns/Transitions:
Scent Article: N/A ☐	Is It: Known ☐ Blind ☐ Dbl Blind ☐
Time on Trail / in Area:	Scent Specific? Yes ☐ No ☐ N/A ☐
DoT confirmed? Yes ☐ No ☐ N/A ☐	Field Tech: N/A ☐

Weather: N/A ☐	Temperature: Indoors ☐
Humidity: Low ☐ Medium ☐ High ☐	Wind Speed:	Direction:

Environment / Conditions:

Notes :

Reward:	Final Trained Response (FTR):

Mapping: North ⬆

Were objectives met?   Yes ☐   No ☐

Training Officer Review: ☐

K-9 TRAINING LOG

Unit ☐	Individual ☐	Demo ☐	Meet/Greet ☐
Date:	Time of Day:	Location:	

Training Objective:

# of Subjects / Hides:	Length/Size of Trail / Area:
Age of Trail/Hide(s):	# Turns/Transitions:
Scent Article: N/A ☐	Is It: Known ☐ Blind ☐ Dbl Blind ☐
Time on Trail / in Area:	Scent Specific? Yes ☐ No ☐ N/A ☐
DoT confirmed? Yes ☐ No ☐ N/A ☐	Field Tech: N/A ☐

Weather: N/A ☐	Temperature: Indoors ☐	
Humidity: Low ☐ Medium ☐ High ☐	Wind Speed:	Direction:

Environment / Conditions:

Notes :

Reward:	Final Trained Response (FTR):

Mapping: *North* ⬆

Were objectives met?   Yes ☐   No ☐

Training Officer Review: ☐

K-9 TRAINING LOG

Unit ☐	Individual ☐	Demo ☐	Meet/Greet ☐

Date:	Time of Day:	Location:

Training Objective:

_____

_____

# of Subjects / Hides:	Length/Size of Trail / Area:
Age of Trail/Hide(s):	# Turns/Transitions:
Scent Article: N/A ☐	Is It: Known ☐ Blind ☐ Dbl Blind ☐
Time on Trail / in Area:	Scent Specific? Yes ☐ No ☐ N/A ☐
DoT confirmed? Yes ☐ No ☐ N/A ☐	Field Tech: N/A ☐

Weather: N/A ☐	Temperature: Indoors ☐
Humidity: Low ☐ Medium ☐ High ☐	Wind Speed:	Direction:

Environment / Conditions: _____

Notes : _____

_____

_____

_____

_____

Reward:	Final Trained Response (FTR):

Mapping: North ⬆

Were objectives met?   Yes ☐   No ☐

Training Officer Review: ☐

K-9 TRAINING LOG

Unit ☐	Individual ☐	Demo ☐	Meet/Greet ☐

Date: _____ | Time of Day: _____ | Location: _____

Training Objective: _____

_____

# of Subjects / Hides:	Length/Size of Trail / Area:
Age of Trail/Hide(s):	# Turns/Transitions:
Scent Article: N/A ☐	Is It: Known ☐ Blind ☐ Dbl Blind ☐
Time on Trail / in Area:	Scent Specific? Yes ☐ No ☐ N/A ☐
DoT confirmed? Yes ☐ No ☐ N/A ☐	Field Tech: N/A ☐

Weather: N/A ☐	Temperature: Indoors ☐
Humidity: Low ☐ Medium ☐ High ☐	Wind Speed:	Direction:

Environment / Conditions: _____

Notes : _____

_____

_____

_____

Reward:	Final Trained Response (FTR):

Mapping: North ↑

Were objectives met?   Yes ☐   No ☐

Training Officer Review: ☐

K-9 TRAINING LOG

Unit ☐	Individual ☐	Demo ☐	Meet/Greet ☐
Date:	Time of Day:	Location:	

Training Objective:

# of Subjects / Hides:	Length/Size of Trail / Area:
Age of Trail/Hide(s):	# Turns/Transitions:
Scent Article: N/A ☐	Is It: Known ☐ Blind ☐ Dbl Blind ☐
Time on Trail / in Area:	Scent Specific? Yes ☐ No ☐ N/A ☐
DoT confirmed? Yes ☐ No ☐ N/A ☐	Field Tech: N/A ☐
Weather: N/A ☐	Temperature: Indoors ☐
Humidity: Low ☐ Medium ☐ High ☐	Wind Speed:	Direction:

Environment / Conditions:

Notes :

Reward: | _Final Trained Response (FTR):_

Mapping: _North_ ⬆

Were objectives met?   Yes ☐   No ☐

Training Officer Review: ☐

K-9 TRAINING LOG

Unit ☐	Individual ☐	Demo ☐	Meet/Greet ☐

Date:	Time of Day:	Location:

Training Objective:

# of Subjects / Hides:	Length/Size of Trail / Area:
Age of Trail/Hide(s):	# Turns/Transitions:
Scent Article: N/A ☐	Is It: Known ☐ Blind ☐ Dbl Blind ☐
Time on Trail / in Area:	Scent Specific? Yes ☐ No ☐ N/A ☐
DoT confirmed? Yes ☐ No ☐ N/A ☐	Field Tech: N/A ☐

Weather: N/A ☐	Temperature: Indoors ☐
Humidity: Low ☐ Medium ☐ High ☐	Wind Speed:	Direction:

Environment / Conditions:

Notes :

Reward:	Final Trained Response (FTR):

Mapping: *North* ⬆

Were objectives met?   Yes ☐   No ☐

Training Officer Review: ☐

K-9 TRAINING LOG

Unit ☐	Individual ☐	Demo ☐	Meet/Greet ☐
Date:	Time of Day:	Location:	

Training Objective:

_____

_____

# of Subjects / Hides:	Length/Size of Trail / Area:
Age of Trail/Hide(s):	# Turns/Transitions:
Scent Article: N/A ☐	Is It: Known ☐ Blind ☐ Dbl Blind ☐
Time on Trail / in Area:	Scent Specific? Yes ☐ No ☐ N/A ☐
DoT confirmed? Yes ☐ No ☐ N/A ☐	Field Tech: N/A ☐

Weather: N/A ☐	Temperature: Indoors ☐
Humidity: Low ☐ Medium ☐ High ☐	Wind Speed:	Direction:

Environment / Conditions: _____

Notes : _____

_____

_____

_____

_____

Reward:	Final Trained Response (FTR):

Mapping: North ⬆

Were objectives met?   Yes ☐   No ☐

Training Officer Review: ☐

K-9 TRAINING LOG

Unit ☐	Individual ☐	Demo ☐	Meet/Greet ☐
Date:	Time of Day:	Location:	

Training Objective:

# of Subjects / Hides:	Length/Size of Trail / Area:
Age of Trail/Hide(s):	# Turns/Transitions:
Scent Article: N/A ☐	Is It: Known ☐ Blind ☐ Dbl Blind ☐
Time on Trail / in Area:	Scent Specific? Yes ☐ No ☐ N/A ☐
DoT confirmed? Yes ☐ No ☐ N/A ☐	Field Tech: N/A ☐

Weather: N/A ☐	Temperature: Indoors ☐
Humidity: Low ☐ Medium ☐ High ☐	Wind Speed:	Direction:

Environment / Conditions:

Notes :

Reward:	Final Trained Response (FTR):

Mapping: North ⬆

Were objectives met?   Yes ☐   No ☐

Training Officer Review: ☐

K-9 TRAINING LOG

Unit ☐	Individual ☐	Demo ☐	Meet/Greet ☐

Date:	Time of Day:	Location:

Training Objective:

_____

_____

# of Subjects / Hides:	Length/Size of Trail / Area:
Age of Trail/Hide(s):	# Turns/Transitions:
Scent Article: N/A ☐	Is It: Known ☐ Blind ☐ Dbl Blind ☐
Time on Trail / in Area:	Scent Specific? Yes ☐ No ☐ N/A ☐
DoT confirmed? Yes ☐ No ☐ N/A ☐	Field Tech: N/A ☐

Weather: N/A ☐	Temperature: Indoors ☐
Humidity: Low ☐ Medium ☐ High ☐	Wind Speed: Direction:

Environment / Conditions:

_____

Notes :

_____

_____

_____

_____

_____

Reward:	Final Trained Response (FTR):

Mapping: *North* ↑

Were objectives met?   Yes ☐   No ☐

Training Officer Review: ☐

K-9 TRAINING LOG

Unit ☐	Individual ☐	Demo ☐	Meet/Greet ☐

Date:	Time of Day:	Location:

Training Objective:

_____

_____

# of Subjects / Hides:	Length/Size of Trail / Area:
Age of Trail/Hide(s):	# Turns/Transitions:
Scent Article: N/A ☐	Is It: Known ☐ Blind ☐ Dbl Blind ☐
Time on Trail / in Area:	Scent Specific? Yes ☐ No ☐ N/A ☐
DoT confirmed? Yes ☐ No ☐ N/A ☐	Field Tech: N/A ☐
Weather: N/A ☐	Temperature: Indoors ☐
Humidity: Low ☐ Medium ☐ High ☐	Wind Speed:	Direction:

Environment / Conditions:

_____

Notes :

_____

_____

_____

_____

Reward:	Final Trained Response (FTR):

Mapping: *North* ⬆

Were objectives met?   Yes ☐   No ☐

Training Officer Review: ☐

K-9 TRAINING LOG

Unit ☐	Individual ☐	Demo ☐	Meet/Greet ☐

Date:	Time of Day:	Location:

Training Objective:
_____

_____

# of Subjects / Hides:	Length/Size of Trail / Area:
Age of Trail/Hide(s):	# Turns/Transitions:
Scent Article: N/A ☐	Is It: Known ☐ Blind ☐ Dbl Blind ☐
Time on Trail / in Area:	Scent Specific? Yes ☐ No ☐ N/A ☐
DoT confirmed? Yes ☐ No ☐ N/A ☐	Field Tech: N/A ☐

Weather: N/A ☐	Temperature: Indoors ☐
Humidity: Low ☐ Medium ☐ High ☐	Wind Speed:	Direction:

Environment / Conditions: _____

Notes : _____

_____

_____

_____

_____

Reward:	Final Trained Response (FTR):

Mapping: *North* ↑

Were objectives met?   Yes ☐   No ☐

Training Officer Review: ☐

K-9 TRAINING LOG

Unit ☐	Individual ☐	Demo ☐	Meet/Greet ☐

Date:	Time of Day:	Location:

Training Objective:

# of Subjects / Hides:	Length/Size of Trail / Area:
Age of Trail/Hide(s):	# Turns/Transitions:
Scent Article: N/A ☐	Is It: Known ☐ Blind ☐ Dbl Blind ☐
Time on Trail / in Area:	Scent Specific? Yes ☐ No ☐ N/A ☐
DoT confirmed? Yes ☐ No ☐ N/A ☐	Field Tech: N/A ☐

Weather: N/A ☐	Temperature: Indoors ☐
Humidity: Low ☐ Medium ☐ High ☐	Wind Speed:	Direction:

Environment / Conditions:

Notes :

Reward:	Final Trained Response (FTR):

Mapping: North ↑

Were objectives met?   Yes ☐   No ☐

Training Officer Review: ☐

K-9 TRAINING LOG

Unit ☐	Individual ☐	Demo ☐	Meet/Greet ☐
Date:	Time of Day:	Location:	

Training Objective:

# of Subjects / Hides:	Length/Size of Trail / Area:
Age of Trail/Hide(s):	# Turns/Transitions:
Scent Article: N/A ☐	Is It: Known ☐ Blind ☐ Dbl Blind ☐
Time on Trail / in Area:	Scent Specific? Yes ☐ No ☐ N/A ☐
DoT confirmed? Yes ☐ No ☐ N/A ☐	Field Tech: N/A ☐

Weather: N/A ☐	Temperature: Indoors ☐
Humidity: Low ☐ Medium ☐ High ☐	Wind Speed:	Direction:

Environment / Conditions:

Notes :

Reward:	Final Trained Response (FTR):

Mapping: *North* ⬆

Were objectives met?   Yes ☐   No ☐

Training Officer Review: ☐

K-9 TRAINING LOG

Unit ☐	Individual ☐	Demo ☐	Meet/Greet ☐
Date:	Time of Day:	Location:	

Training Objective:

# of Subjects / Hides:	Length/Size of Trail / Area:
Age of Trail/Hide(s):	# Turns/Transitions:
Scent Article: N/A ☐	Is It: Known ☐ Blind ☐ Dbl Blind ☐
Time on Trail / in Area:	Scent Specific? Yes ☐ No ☐ N/A ☐
DoT confirmed? Yes ☐ No ☐ N/A ☐	Field Tech: N/A ☐

Weather: N/A ☐	Temperature: Indoors ☐
Humidity: Low ☐ Medium ☐ High ☐	Wind Speed:	Direction:

Environment / Conditions:

Notes :

Reward:	Final Trained Response (FTR):

Mapping: North ↑

Were objectives met?   Yes ☐   No ☐

Training Officer Review: ☐

K-9 TRAINING LOG

Unit ☐	Individual ☐	Demo ☐	Meet/Greet ☐

Date: | Time of Day: | Location:

Training Objective:

_____

_____

# of Subjects / Hides:	Length/Size of Trail / Area:
Age of Trail/Hide(s):	# Turns/Transitions:
Scent Article: N/A ☐	Is It: Known ☐ Blind ☐ Dbl Blind ☐
Time on Trail / in Area:	Scent Specific? Yes ☐ No ☐ N/A ☐
DoT confirmed? Yes ☐ No ☐ N/A ☐	Field Tech: N/A ☐

Weather: N/A ☐	Temperature: Indoors ☐
Humidity: Low ☐ Medium ☐ High ☐	Wind Speed:	Direction:

Environment / Conditions: _____

Notes :

_____

_____

_____

_____

Reward:	Final Trained Response (FTR):

Mapping: North ⬆

Were objectives met? Yes ☐ No ☐

Training Officer Review: ☐

K-9 TRAINING LOG

Unit ☐	Individual ☐	Demo ☐	Meet/Greet ☐

Date:	Time of Day:	Location:

Training Objective:

_____

_____

# of Subjects / Hides:	Length/Size of Trail / Area:
Age of Trail/Hide(s):	# Turns/Transitions:
Scent Article: N/A ☐	Is It: Known ☐ Blind ☐ Dbl Blind ☐
Time on Trail / in Area:	Scent Specific? Yes ☐ No ☐ N/A ☐
DoT confirmed? Yes ☐ No ☐ N/A ☐	Field Tech: N/A ☐

Weather: N/A ☐	Temperature: Indoors ☐
Humidity: Low ☐ Medium ☐ High ☐	Wind Speed: Direction:

Environment / Conditions: _____

Notes : _____

_____

_____

_____

_____

Reward:	Final Trained Response (FTR):

Mapping: *North* ↑

Were objectives met?   Yes ☐   No ☐

Training Officer Review: ☐

K-9 TRAINING LOG

Unit ☐	Individual ☐	Demo ☐	Meet/Greet ☐
Date:	Time of Day:	Location:	

Training Objective:

# of Subjects / Hides:	Length/Size of Trail / Area:
Age of Trail/Hide(s):	# Turns/Transitions:
Scent Article: N/A ☐	Is It: Known ☐ Blind ☐ Dbl Blind ☐
Time on Trail / in Area:	Scent Specific? Yes ☐ No ☐ N/A ☐
DoT confirmed? Yes ☐ No ☐ N/A ☐	Field Tech: N/A ☐

Weather: N/A ☐	Temperature: Indoors ☐
Humidity: Low ☐ Medium ☐ High ☐	Wind Speed: Direction:
Environment / Conditions:	

Notes :

Reward:	Final Trained Response (FTR):

Mapping: *North* ↑

Were objectives met?   Yes ☐   No ☐

Training Officer Review: ☐

K-9 TRAINING LOG

Unit ☐	Individual ☐	Demo ☐	Meet/Greet ☐

Date:	Time of Day:	Location:

Training Objective:

_____

_____

# of Subjects / Hides:		Length/Size of Trail / Area:
Age of Trail/Hide(s):		# Turns/Transitions:
Scent Article:	N/A ☐	Is It: Known ☐ Blind ☐ Dbl Blind ☐
Time on Trail / in Area:		Scent Specific? Yes ☐ No ☐ N/A ☐
DoT confirmed? Yes ☐ No ☐ N/A ☐		Field Tech: N/A ☐

Weather: N/A ☐	Temperature: Indoors ☐
Humidity: Low ☐ Medium ☐ High ☐	Wind Speed:	Direction:

Environment / Conditions: _____

_____

Notes : _____

_____

_____

_____

_____

Reward:	*Final Trained Response (FTR):*

Mapping: *North* ↑

Were objectives met?   Yes ☐   No ☐

Training Officer Review: ☐

K-9 TRAINING LOG

Unit ☐	Individual ☐	Demo ☐	Meet/Greet ☐
Date:	Time of Day:	Location:	

Training Objective:

# of Subjects / Hides:	Length/Size of Trail / Area:
Age of Trail/Hide(s):	# Turns/Transitions:
Scent Article: N/A ☐	Is It: Known ☐ Blind ☐ Dbl Blind ☐
Time on Trail / in Area:	Scent Specific? Yes ☐ No ☐ N/A ☐
DoT confirmed? Yes ☐ No ☐ N/A ☐	Field Tech: N/A ☐
Weather: N/A ☐	Temperature: Indoors ☐
Humidity: Low ☐ Medium ☐ High ☐	Wind Speed:	Direction:

Environment / Conditions:

Notes :

Reward:	Final Trained Response (FTR):

Mapping: North ↑

Were objectives met?   Yes ☐   No ☐

Training Officer Review: ☐

K-9 TRAINING LOG

Unit ☐	Individual ☐	Demo ☐	Meet/Greet ☐
Date:	Time of Day:	Location:	

Training Objective:

# of Subjects / Hides:	Length/Size of Trail / Area:
Age of Trail/Hide(s):	# Turns/Transitions:
Scent Article: N/A ☐	Is It: Known ☐ Blind ☐ Dbl Blind ☐
Time on Trail / in Area:	Scent Specific? Yes ☐ No ☐ N/A ☐
DoT confirmed? Yes ☐ No ☐ N/A ☐	Field Tech: N/A ☐

Weather: N/A ☐	Temperature: Indoors ☐	
Humidity: Low ☐ Medium ☐ High ☐	Wind Speed:	Direction:
Environment / Conditions:		

Notes :

Reward: | *Final Trained Response (FTR):*

Mapping: *North* ↑

Were objectives met?   Yes ☐   No ☐

Training Officer Review: ☐

K-9 TRAINING LOG

Unit ☐	Individual ☐	Demo ☐	Meet/Greet ☐

Date:	Time of Day:	Location:

Training Objective:

# of Subjects / Hides:	Length/Size of Trail / Area:
Age of Trail/Hide(s):	# Turns/Transitions:
Scent Article: N/A ☐	Is It: Known ☐ Blind ☐ Dbl Blind ☐
Time on Trail / in Area:	Scent Specific? Yes ☐ No ☐ N/A ☐
DoT confirmed? Yes ☐ No ☐ N/A ☐	Field Tech: N/A ☐

Weather: N/A ☐	Temperature: Indoors ☐
Humidity: Low ☐ Medium ☐ High ☐	Wind Speed:	Direction:

Environment / Conditions:

Notes :

Reward:	Final Trained Response (FTR):

Mapping: North ↑

Were objectives met?   Yes ☐   No ☐

Training Officer Review: ☐

K-9 TRAINING LOG

Unit ☐	Individual ☐	Demo ☐	Meet/Greet ☐

Date:	Time of Day:	Location:

Training Objective:

# of Subjects / Hides:	Length/Size of Trail / Area:
Age of Trail/Hide(s):	# Turns/Transitions:
Scent Article: N/A ☐	Is It: Known ☐ Blind ☐ Dbl Blind ☐
Time on Trail / in Area:	Scent Specific? Yes ☐ No ☐ N/A ☐
DoT confirmed? Yes ☐ No ☐ N/A ☐	Field Tech: N/A ☐

Weather: N/A ☐	Temperature: Indoors ☐
Humidity: Low ☐ Medium ☐ High ☐	Wind Speed: Direction:

Environment / Conditions:

Notes :

Reward:	Final Trained Response (FTR):

Mapping: North ↑

Were objectives met?   Yes ☐   No ☐

Training Officer Review: ☐

K-9 TRAINING LOG

Unit ☐	Individual ☐	Demo ☐	Meet/Greet ☐

Date: | Time of Day: | Location:

Training Objective:

# of Subjects / Hides:	Length/Size of Trail / Area:
Age of Trail/Hide(s):	# Turns/Transitions:
Scent Article: N/A ☐	Is It: Known ☐ Blind ☐ Dbl Blind ☐
Time on Trail / in Area:	Scent Specific? Yes ☐ No ☐ N/A ☐
DoT confirmed? Yes ☐ No ☐ N/A ☐	Field Tech: N/A ☐
Weather: N/A ☐	Temperature: Indoors ☐
Humidity: Low ☐ Medium ☐ High ☐	Wind Speed:	Direction:

Environment / Conditions:

Notes :

Reward: | *Final Trained Response (FTR):*

Mapping: *North* ⬆

Were objectives met?   Yes ☐   No ☐

Training Officer Review: ☐

K-9 TRAINING LOG

Unit ☐	Individual ☐	Demo ☐	Meet/Greet ☐

Date:	Time of Day:	Location:

Training Objective:

# of Subjects / Hides:	Length/Size of Trail / Area:
Age of Trail/Hide(s):	# Turns/Transitions:
Scent Article: N/A ☐	Is It: Known ☐ Blind ☐ Dbl Blind ☐
Time on Trail / in Area:	Scent Specific? Yes ☐ No ☐ N/A ☐
DoT confirmed? Yes ☐ No ☐ N/A ☐	Field Tech: N/A ☐

Weather: N/A ☐	Temperature: Indoors ☐
Humidity: Low ☐ Medium ☐ High ☐	Wind Speed:	Direction:

Environment / Conditions:

Notes :

Reward:	*Final Trained Response (FTR):*

Mapping: *North* ⬆

Were objectives met?   Yes ☐   No ☐

Training Officer Review: ☐

K-9 TRAINING LOG

Unit ☐	Individual ☐	Demo ☐	Meet/Greet ☐

Date: | Time of Day: | Location:

Training Objective:

# of Subjects / Hides:	Length/Size of Trail / Area:
Age of Trail/Hide(s):	# Turns/Transitions:
Scent Article: N/A ☐	Is It: Known ☐ Blind ☐ Dbl Blind ☐
Time on Trail / in Area:	Scent Specific? Yes ☐ No ☐ N/A ☐
DoT confirmed? Yes ☐ No ☐ N/A ☐	Field Tech: N/A ☐

Weather: N/A ☐	Temperature: Indoors ☐
Humidity: Low ☐ Medium ☐ High ☐	Wind Speed:	Direction:

Environment / Conditions:

Notes :

Reward:	Final Trained Response (FTR):

Mapping: *North* ⬆

Were objectives met?   Yes ☐   No ☐

Training Officer Review: ☐

K-9 TRAINING LOG

Unit ☐	Individual ☐	Demo ☐	Meet/Greet ☐
Date:	Time of Day:	Location:	

Training Objective:

# of Subjects / Hides:	Length/Size of Trail / Area:
Age of Trail/Hide(s):	# Turns/Transitions:
Scent Article: N/A ☐	Is It: Known ☐ Blind ☐ Dbl Blind ☐
Time on Trail / in Area:	Scent Specific? Yes ☐ No ☐ N/A ☐
DoT confirmed? Yes ☐ No ☐ N/A ☐	Field Tech: N/A ☐

Weather: N/A ☐	Temperature:	Indoors ☐
Humidity: Low ☐ Medium ☐ High ☐	Wind Speed:	Direction:
Environment / Conditions:		

Notes :

Reward:	Final Trained Response (FTR):

Mapping: *North* ↑

Were objectives met? Yes ☐ No ☐

Training Officer Review: ☐

K-9 TRAINING LOG

Unit ☐	Individual ☐	Demo ☐	Meet/Greet ☐

Date:	Time of Day:	Location:

Training Objective:

# of Subjects / Hides:	Length/Size of Trail / Area:
Age of Trail/Hide(s):	# Turns/Transitions:
Scent Article: N/A ☐	Is It: Known ☐ Blind ☐ Dbl Blind ☐
Time on Trail / in Area:	Scent Specific? Yes ☐ No ☐ N/A ☐
DoT confirmed? Yes ☐ No ☐ N/A ☐	Field Tech: N/A ☐

Weather: N/A ☐	Temperature: Indoors ☐
Humidity: Low ☐ Medium ☐ High ☐	Wind Speed:	Direction:

Environment / Conditions:

Notes :

Reward:	Final Trained Response (FTR):

Mapping: North ⬆

Were objectives met?   Yes ☐   No ☐

Training Officer Review: ☐

K-9 TRAINING LOG

Unit ☐	Individual ☐	Demo ☐	Meet/Greet ☐

Date:	Time of Day:	Location:

Training Objective:

# of Subjects / Hides:	Length/Size of Trail / Area:
Age of Trail/Hide(s):	# Turns/Transitions:
Scent Article: N/A ☐	Is It: Known ☐ Blind ☐ Dbl Blind ☐
Time on Trail / in Area:	Scent Specific? Yes ☐ No ☐ N/A ☐
DoT confirmed? Yes ☐ No ☐ N/A ☐	Field Tech: N/A ☐

Weather: N/A ☐	Temperature: Indoors ☐
Humidity: Low ☐ Medium ☐ High ☐	Wind Speed: Direction:

Environment / Conditions:

Notes :

Reward:	Final Trained Response (FTR):

Mapping: *North* ↑

Were objectives met?   Yes ☐   No ☐

Training Officer Review: ☐

K-9 TRAINING LOG

Unit ☐	Individual ☐	Demo ☐	Meet/Greet ☐
Date:	Time of Day:	Location:	

Training Objective:

# of Subjects / Hides:	Length/Size of Trail / Area:
Age of Trail/Hide(s):	# Turns/Transitions:
Scent Article: N/A ☐	Is It: Known ☐ Blind ☐ Dbl Blind ☐
Time on Trail / in Area:	Scent Specific? Yes ☐ No ☐ N/A ☐
DoT confirmed? Yes ☐ No ☐ N/A ☐	Field Tech: N/A ☐

Weather: N/A ☐	Temperature: Indoors ☐
Humidity: Low ☐ Medium ☐ High ☐	Wind Speed:	Direction:

Environment / Conditions:

Notes :

Reward:	Final Trained Response (FTR):

Mapping: North ↑

Were objectives met?   Yes ☐   No ☐

Training Officer Review: ☐

K-9 TRAINING LOG

Unit ☐	Individual ☐	Demo ☐	Meet/Greet ☐

Date:	Time of Day:	Location:

Training Objective:

# of Subjects / Hides:	Length/Size of Trail / Area:
Age of Trail/Hide(s):	# Turns/Transitions:
Scent Article: N/A ☐	Is It: Known ☐ Blind ☐ Dbl Blind ☐
Time on Trail / in Area:	Scent Specific? Yes ☐ No ☐ N/A ☐
DoT confirmed? Yes ☐ No ☐ N/A ☐	Field Tech: N/A ☐

Weather: N/A ☐	Temperature: Indoors ☐
Humidity: Low ☐ Medium ☐ High ☐	Wind Speed:	Direction:

Environment / Conditions:

Notes :

Reward:	Final Trained Response (FTR):

Mapping: North ↑

Were objectives met?   Yes ☐   No ☐

Training Officer Review: ☐

K-9 TRAINING LOG

Unit ☐	Individual ☐	Demo ☐	Meet/Greet ☐

Date:	Time of Day:	Location:

Training Objective:

# of Subjects / Hides:	Length/Size of Trail / Area:
Age of Trail/Hide(s):	# Turns/Transitions:
Scent Article: N/A ☐	Is It: Known ☐ Blind ☐ Dbl Blind ☐
Time on Trail / in Area:	Scent Specific? Yes ☐ No ☐ N/A ☐
DoT confirmed? Yes ☐ No ☐ N/A ☐	Field Tech: N/A ☐

Weather: N/A ☐	Temperature: Indoors ☐
Humidity: Low ☐ Medium ☐ High ☐	Wind Speed: Direction:
Environment / Conditions:	

Notes :

Reward:	Final Trained Response (FTR):

Mapping: North ↑

Were objectives met?   Yes ☐   No ☐

Training Officer Review: ☐

K-9 TRAINING LOG

Unit ☐	Individual ☐	Demo ☐	Meet/Greet ☐
Date:	Time of Day:	Location:	

Training Objective:

# of Subjects / Hides:		Length/Size of Trail / Area:		
Age of Trail/Hide(s):		# Turns/Transitions:		
Scent Article:	N/A ☐	Is It: Known ☐ Blind ☐ Dbl Blind ☐		
Time on Trail / in Area:		Scent Specific? Yes ☐ No ☐ N/A ☐		
DoT confirmed? Yes ☐ No ☐ N/A ☐		Field Tech: N/A ☐		

Weather:	N/A ☐	Temperature:	Indoors ☐
Humidity: Low ☐ Medium ☐ High ☐		Wind Speed:	Direction:
Environment / Conditions:			

Notes :

Reward:	Final Trained Response (FTR):

Mapping: North ↑

Were objectives met?   Yes ☐   No ☐

Training Officer Review: ☐

K-9 TRAINING LOG

Unit ☐	Individual ☐	Demo ☐	Meet/Greet ☐
Date:	Time of Day:	Location:	

Training Objective:

# of Subjects / Hides:	Length/Size of Trail / Area:
Age of Trail/Hide(s):	# Turns/Transitions:
Scent Article: N/A ☐	Is It: Known ☐ Blind ☐ Dbl Blind ☐
Time on Trail / in Area:	Scent Specific? Yes ☐ No ☐ N/A ☐
DoT confirmed? Yes ☐ No ☐ N/A ☐	Field Tech: N/A ☐

Weather: N/A ☐	Temperature: Indoors ☐
Humidity: Low ☐ Medium ☐ High ☐	Wind Speed:	Direction:

Environment / Conditions:

Notes :

Reward:	Final Trained Response (FTR):

Mapping: North ↑

Were objectives met?   Yes ☐   No ☐

Training Officer Review: ☐

K-9 TRAINING LOG

Unit ☐	Individual ☐	Demo ☐	Meet/Greet ☐

Date:	Time of Day:	Location:

Training Objective:

# of Subjects / Hides:	Length/Size of Trail / Area:
Age of Trail/Hide(s):	# Turns/Transitions:
Scent Article: N/A ☐	Is It: Known ☐ Blind ☐ Dbl Blind ☐
Time on Trail / in Area:	Scent Specific? Yes ☐ No ☐ N/A ☐
DoT confirmed? Yes ☐ No ☐ N/A ☐	Field Tech: N/A ☐

Weather: N/A ☐	Temperature: Indoors ☐
Humidity: Low ☐ Medium ☐ High ☐	Wind Speed: Direction:

Environment / Conditions:

Notes :

Reward:	Final Trained Response (FTR):

Mapping: *North* ↑

Were objectives met?   Yes ☐   No ☐

Training Officer Review: ☐

K-9 TRAINING LOG

Unit ☐	Individual ☐	Demo ☐	Meet/Greet ☐

Date:	Time of Day:	Location:

Training Objective:

_____

_____

# of Subjects / Hides:	Length/Size of Trail / Area:
Age of Trail/Hide(s):	# Turns/Transitions:
Scent Article: N/A ☐	Is It: Known ☐ Blind ☐ Dbl Blind ☐
Time on Trail / in Area:	Scent Specific? Yes ☐ No ☐ N/A ☐
DoT confirmed? Yes ☐ No ☐ N/A ☐	Field Tech: N/A ☐

Weather: N/A ☐	Temperature: Indoors ☐
Humidity: Low ☐ Medium ☐ High ☐	Wind Speed:	Direction:

Environment / Conditions:

_____

Notes :

_____

_____

_____

_____

_____

Reward:	*Final Trained Response (FTR):*

Mapping: *North* ⬆

Were objectives met?   Yes ☐   No ☐

Training Officer Review: ☐

K-9 TRAINING LOG

Unit ☐	Individual ☐	Demo ☐	Meet/Greet ☐
Date:	Time of Day:	Location:	

Training Objective:

# of Subjects / Hides:	Length/Size of Trail / Area:
Age of Trail/Hide(s):	# Turns/Transitions:
Scent Article: N/A ☐	Is It: Known ☐ Blind ☐ Dbl Blind ☐
Time on Trail / in Area:	Scent Specific? Yes ☐ No ☐ N/A ☐
DoT confirmed? Yes ☐ No ☐ N/A ☐	Field Tech: N/A ☐

Weather: N/A ☐	Temperature: Indoors ☐
Humidity: Low ☐ Medium ☐ High ☐	Wind Speed:	Direction:

Environment / Conditions:

Notes :

Reward:	Final Trained Response (FTR):

Mapping: North ↑

Were objectives met?   Yes ☐ No ☐

Training Officer Review: ☐

K-9 TRAINING LOG

Unit ☐	Individual ☐	Demo ☐	Meet/Greet ☐

Date: | Time of Day: | Location:

Training Objective:

_____

_____

# of Subjects / Hides:	Length/Size of Trail / Area:
Age of Trail/Hide(s):	# Turns/Transitions:
Scent Article: N/A ☐	Is It: Known ☐ Blind ☐ Dbl Blind ☐
Time on Trail / in Area:	Scent Specific? Yes ☐ No ☐ N/A ☐
DoT confirmed? Yes ☐ No ☐ N/A ☐	Field Tech: N/A ☐
Weather: N/A ☐	Temperature: Indoors ☐
Humidity: Low ☐ Medium ☐ High ☐	Wind Speed:	Direction:
Environment / Conditions:		

_____

Notes :

_____

_____

_____

_____

Reward:	Final Trained Response (FTR):

Mapping: North ↑

Were objectives met?   Yes ☐   No ☐

Training Officer Review: ☐

K-9 TRAINING LOG

Unit ☐	Individual ☐	Demo ☐	Meet/Greet ☐
Date:	Time of Day:	Location:	

Training Objective:

# of Subjects / Hides:	Length/Size of Trail / Area:
Age of Trail/Hide(s):	# Turns/Transitions:
Scent Article: N/A ☐	Is It: Known ☐ Blind ☐ Dbl Blind ☐
Time on Trail / in Area:	Scent Specific? Yes ☐ No ☐ N/A ☐
DoT confirmed? Yes ☐ No ☐ N/A ☐	Field Tech: N/A ☐

Weather: N/A ☐	Temperature: Indoors ☐
Humidity: Low ☐ Medium ☐ High ☐	Wind Speed:	Direction:

Environment / Conditions:

Notes :

Reward:	Final Trained Response (FTR):

Mapping: North ↑

Were objectives met?   Yes ☐   No ☐

Training Officer Review: ☐

K-9 TRAINING LOG

Unit ☐	Individual ☐	Demo ☐	Meet/Greet ☐

Date:	Time of Day:	Location:

Training Objective:

# of Subjects / Hides:	Length/Size of Trail / Area:
Age of Trail/Hide(s):	# Turns/Transitions:
Scent Article: N/A ☐	Is It: Known ☐ Blind ☐ Dbl Blind ☐
Time on Trail / in Area:	Scent Specific? Yes ☐ No ☐ N/A ☐
DoT confirmed? Yes ☐ No ☐ N/A ☐	Field Tech: N/A ☐

Weather: N/A ☐	Temperature: Indoors ☐
Humidity: Low ☐ Medium ☐ High ☐	Wind Speed: Direction:

Environment / Conditions:

Notes :

Reward:	Final Trained Response (FTR):

Mapping: *North* ⬆

Were objectives met?   Yes ☐   No ☐

Training Officer Review: ☐

K-9 TRAINING LOG

Unit ☐	Individual ☐	Demo ☐	Meet/Greet ☐

Date:	Time of Day:	Location:

Training Objective:

_____

_____

# of Subjects / Hides:	Length/Size of Trail / Area:
Age of Trail/Hide(s):	# Turns/Transitions:
Scent Article: N/A ☐	Is It: Known ☐ Blind ☐ Dbl Blind ☐
Time on Trail / in Area:	Scent Specific? Yes ☐ No ☐ N/A ☐
DoT confirmed? Yes ☐ No ☐ N/A ☐	Field Tech: N/A ☐

Weather: N/A ☐	Temperature: Indoors ☐
Humidity: Low ☐ Medium ☐ High ☐	Wind Speed:	Direction:
Environment / Conditions:	

_____

Notes :

_____

_____

_____

_____

Reward:	Final Trained Response (FTR):

Mapping: North ⬆

Were objectives met?   Yes ☐   No ☐

Training Officer Review: ☐

K-9 TRAINING LOG

Unit ☐	Individual ☐	Demo ☐	Meet/Greet ☐
Date:	Time of Day:	Location:	

Training Objective:
_____
_____

# of Subjects / Hides:	Length/Size of Trail / Area:
Age of Trail/Hide(s):	# Turns/Transitions:
Scent Article: N/A ☐	Is It: Known ☐ Blind ☐ Dbl Blind ☐
Time on Trail / in Area:	Scent Specific? Yes ☐ No ☐ N/A ☐
DoT confirmed? Yes ☐ No ☐ N/A ☐	Field Tech: N/A ☐

Weather: N/A ☐	Temperature: Indoors ☐
Humidity: Low ☐ Medium ☐ High ☐	Wind Speed: Direction:

Environment / Conditions:
_____

Notes :
_____
_____
_____
_____
_____

Reward:	Final Trained Response (FTR):

Mapping: North ↑

Were objectives met?   Yes ☐   No ☐

Training Officer Review: ☐

K-9 TRAINING LOG

Unit ☐	Individual ☐	Demo ☐	Meet/Greet ☐

Date: | Time of Day: | Location:

Training Objective:

# of Subjects / Hides:	Length/Size of Trail / Area:
Age of Trail/Hide(s):	# Turns/Transitions:
Scent Article: N/A ☐	Is It: Known ☐ Blind ☐ Dbl Blind ☐
Time on Trail / in Area:	Scent Specific? Yes ☐ No ☐ N/A ☐
DoT confirmed? Yes ☐ No ☐ N/A ☐	Field Tech: N/A ☐

Weather: N/A ☐	Temperature: Indoors ☐
Humidity: Low ☐ Medium ☐ High ☐	Wind Speed:	Direction:

Environment / Conditions:

Notes :

Reward:	*Final Trained Response (FTR):*

Mapping: *North* ↑

Were objectives met?   Yes ☐ No ☐

Training Officer Review: ☐

K-9 TRAINING LOG

Unit ☐	Individual ☐	Demo ☐	Meet/Greet ☐
Date:	Time of Day:	Location:	

Training Objective:

# of Subjects / Hides:	Length/Size of Trail / Area:
Age of Trail/Hide(s):	# Turns/Transitions:
Scent Article: N/A ☐	Is It: Known ☐ Blind ☐ Dbl Blind ☐
Time on Trail / in Area:	Scent Specific? Yes ☐ No ☐ N/A ☐
DoT confirmed? Yes ☐ No ☐ N/A ☐	Field Tech: N/A ☐

Weather: N/A ☐	Temperature: Indoors ☐
Humidity: Low ☐ Medium ☐ High ☐	Wind Speed:	Direction:

Environment / Conditions:

Notes :

Reward:	Final Trained Response (FTR):

Mapping: North ⬆

Were objectives met?   Yes ☐ No ☐

Training Officer Review: ☐

K-9 TRAINING LOG

Unit ☐	Individual ☐	Demo ☐	Meet/Greet ☐
Date:	Time of Day:	Location:	

Training Objective:

# of Subjects / Hides:	Length/Size of Trail / Area:
Age of Trail/Hide(s):	# Turns/Transitions:
Scent Article: N/A ☐	Is It: Known ☐ Blind ☐ Dbl Blind ☐
Time on Trail / in Area:	Scent Specific? Yes ☐ No ☐ N/A ☐
DoT confirmed? Yes ☐ No ☐ N/A ☐	Field Tech: N/A ☐
Weather: N/A ☐	Temperature: Indoors ☐
Humidity: Low ☐ Medium ☐ High ☐	Wind Speed: Direction:

Environment / Conditions:

Notes :

Reward:	Final Trained Response (FTR):

Mapping: *North* ↑

Were objectives met?   Yes ☐   No ☐

Training Officer Review: ☐

K-9 TRAINING LOG

Unit ☐	Individual ☐	Demo ☐	Meet/Greet ☐

Date: | Time of Day: | Location:

Training Objective:

_____

_____

# of Subjects / Hides:	Length/Size of Trail / Area:
Age of Trail/Hide(s):	# Turns/Transitions:
Scent Article: N/A ☐	Is It: Known ☐ Blind ☐ Dbl Blind ☐
Time on Trail / in Area:	Scent Specific? Yes ☐ No ☐ N/A ☐
DoT confirmed? Yes ☐ No ☐ N/A ☐	Field Tech: N/A ☐

Weather: N/A ☐	Temperature: Indoors ☐
Humidity: Low ☐ Medium ☐ High ☐	Wind Speed:	Direction:
Environment / Conditions:		

Notes :

_____

_____

_____

_____

_____

Reward:	Final Trained Response (FTR):

Mapping: North ↑

Were objectives met?   Yes ☐   No ☐

Training Officer Review: ☐

K-9 TRAINING LOG

Unit ☐	Individual ☐	Demo ☐	Meet/Greet ☐

Date:	Time of Day:	Location:

Training Objective: _____

_____

# of Subjects / Hides:	Length/Size of Trail / Area:
Age of Trail/Hide(s):	# Turns/Transitions:
Scent Article: N/A ☐	Is It: Known ☐ Blind ☐ Dbl Blind ☐
Time on Trail / in Area:	Scent Specific? Yes ☐ No ☐ N/A ☐
DoT confirmed? Yes ☐ No ☐ N/A ☐	Field Tech: N/A ☐

Weather: N/A ☐	Temperature: Indoors ☐
Humidity: Low ☐ Medium ☐ High ☐	Wind Speed: Direction:

Environment / Conditions: _____

Notes : _____

_____

_____

_____

_____

Reward:	Final Trained Response (FTR):

Mapping: *North* ⬆

Were objectives met?   Yes ☐   No ☐

Training Officer Review: ☐

K-9 TRAINING LOG

Unit ☐	Individual ☐	Demo ☐	Meet/Greet ☐

Date:	Time of Day:	Location:

Training Objective:

_____

_____

# of Subjects / Hides:		Length/Size of Trail / Area:
Age of Trail/Hide(s):		# Turns/Transitions:
Scent Article:	N/A ☐	Is It: Known ☐ Blind ☐ Dbl Blind ☐
Time on Trail / in Area:		Scent Specific? Yes ☐ No ☐ N/A ☐
DoT confirmed? Yes ☐ No ☐	N/A ☐	Field Tech: N/A ☐

Weather:	N/A ☐	Temperature: Indoors ☐
Humidity: Low ☐ Medium ☐ High ☐	Wind Speed:	Direction:

Environment / Conditions: _____

Notes : _____

_____

_____

_____

_____

Reward:	Final Trained Response (FTR):

Mapping: *North* ⬆

Were objectives met?   Yes ☐   No ☐

Training Officer Review: ☐

K-9 TRAINING LOG

Unit ☐	Individual ☐	Demo ☐	Meet/Greet ☐

Date: | Time of Day: | Location:

Training Objective:

_____

_____

# of Subjects / Hides:	Length/Size of Trail / Area:
Age of Trail/Hide(s):	# Turns/Transitions:
Scent Article: N/A ☐	Is It: Known ☐ Blind ☐ Dbl Blind ☐
Time on Trail / in Area:	Scent Specific? Yes ☐ No ☐ N/A ☐
DoT confirmed? Yes ☐ No ☐ N/A ☐	Field Tech: N/A ☐

Weather: N/A ☐	Temperature:	Indoors ☐
Humidity: Low ☐ Medium ☐ High ☐	Wind Speed:	Direction:

Environment / Conditions: _____

Notes : _____

_____

_____

_____

_____

Reward:	Final Trained Response (FTR):

Mapping: *North* ↑

Were objectives met?   Yes ☐   No ☐

Training Officer Review: ☐

K-9 TRAINING LOG

Unit ☐	Individual ☐	Demo ☐	Meet/Greet ☐

Date:	Time of Day:	Location:

Training Objective:

# of Subjects / Hides:	Length/Size of Trail / Area:
Age of Trail/Hide(s):	# Turns/Transitions:
Scent Article: N/A ☐	Is It: Known ☐ Blind ☐ Dbl Blind ☐
Time on Trail / in Area:	Scent Specific? Yes ☐ No ☐ N/A ☐
DoT confirmed? Yes ☐ No ☐ N/A ☐	Field Tech: N/A ☐

Weather: N/A ☐	Temperature: Indoors ☐
Humidity: Low ☐ Medium ☐ High ☐	Wind Speed:	Direction:

Environment / Conditions:

Notes :

Reward:	Final Trained Response (FTR):

Mapping: *North* ↑

Were objectives met?   Yes ☐   No ☐

Training Officer Review: ☐

K-9 TRAINING LOG

Unit ☐	Individual ☐	Demo ☐	Meet/Greet ☐
Date:	Time of Day:	Location:	

Training Objective:

# of Subjects / Hides:	Length/Size of Trail / Area:
Age of Trail/Hide(s):	# Turns/Transitions:
Scent Article: N/A ☐	Is It: Known ☐ Blind ☐ Dbl Blind ☐
Time on Trail / in Area:	Scent Specific? Yes ☐ No ☐ N/A ☐
DoT confirmed? Yes ☐ No ☐ N/A ☐	Field Tech: N/A ☐

Weather: N/A ☐	Temperature: Indoors ☐
Humidity: Low ☐ Medium ☐ High ☐	Wind Speed:	Direction:

Environment / Conditions:

Notes :

Reward:	Final Trained Response (FTR):

Mapping: North ⬆

Were objectives met?   Yes ☐ No ☐

Training Officer Review: ☐

K-9 TRAINING LOG

Unit ☐	Individual ☐	Demo ☐	Meet/Greet ☐

Date:	Time of Day:	Location:

Training Objective:

# of Subjects / Hides:	Length/Size of Trail / Area:
Age of Trail/Hide(s):	# Turns/Transitions:
Scent Article: N/A ☐	Is It: Known ☐ Blind ☐ Dbl Blind ☐
Time on Trail / in Area:	Scent Specific? Yes ☐ No ☐ N/A ☐
DoT confirmed? Yes ☐ No ☐ N/A ☐	Field Tech: N/A ☐

Weather: N/A ☐	Temperature: Indoors ☐
Humidity: Low ☐ Medium ☐ High ☐	Wind Speed: Direction:

Environment / Conditions:

Notes :

Reward:	Final Trained Response (FTR):

Mapping: *North* ⬆

Were objectives met?   Yes ☐   No ☐

Training Officer Review: ☐

K-9 TRAINING LOG

Unit ☐	Individual ☐	Demo ☐	Meet/Greet ☐

Date: | Time of Day: | Location:

Training Objective: _____

_____

# of Subjects / Hides:	Length/Size of Trail / Area:
Age of Trail/Hide(s):	# Turns/Transitions:
Scent Article: N/A ☐	Is It: Known ☐ Blind ☐ Dbl Blind ☐
Time on Trail / in Area:	Scent Specific? Yes ☐ No ☐ N/A ☐
DoT confirmed? Yes ☐ No ☐ N/A ☐	Field Tech: N/A ☐

Weather: N/A ☐	Temperature:	Indoors ☐
Humidity: Low ☐ Medium ☐ High ☐	Wind Speed:	Direction:
Environment / Conditions:		

Notes : _____

_____

_____

_____

_____

Reward:	Final Trained Response (FTR):

Mapping: North ⬆

Were objectives met?   Yes ☐   No ☐

Training Officer Review: ☐

K-9 TRAINING LOG

Unit ☐	Individual ☐	Demo ☐	Meet/Greet ☐

Date: Time of Day: Location:

Training Objective:

# of Subjects / Hides:	Length/Size of Trail / Area:
Age of Trail/Hide(s):	# Turns/Transitions:
Scent Article: N/A ☐	Is It: Known ☐ Blind ☐ Dbl Blind ☐
Time on Trail / in Area:	Scent Specific? Yes ☐ No ☐ N/A ☐
DoT confirmed? Yes ☐ No ☐ N/A ☐	Field Tech: N/A ☐
Weather: N/A ☐	Temperature: Indoors ☐
Humidity: Low ☐ Medium ☐ High ☐	Wind Speed: Direction:

Environment / Conditions:

Notes :

Reward: *Final Trained Response (FTR):*

Mapping: *North* ↑

Were objectives met?   Yes ☐   No ☐

Training Officer Review: ☐

K-9 TRAINING LOG

Unit ☐	Individual ☐	Demo ☐	Meet/Greet ☐

Date:	Time of Day:	Location:

Training Objective:

# of Subjects / Hides:	Length/Size of Trail / Area:
Age of Trail/Hide(s):	# Turns/Transitions:
Scent Article: N/A ☐	Is It: Known ☐ Blind ☐ Dbl Blind ☐
Time on Trail / in Area:	Scent Specific? Yes ☐ No ☐ N/A ☐
DoT confirmed? Yes ☐ No ☐ N/A ☐	Field Tech: N/A ☐

Weather: N/A ☐	Temperature:	Indoors ☐
Humidity: Low ☐ Medium ☐ High ☐	Wind Speed:	Direction:

Environment / Conditions:

Notes :

Reward:	Final Trained Response (FTR):

Mapping: *North* ⬆

Were objectives met?   Yes ☐   No ☐

Training Officer Review: ☐

K-9 TRAINING LOG

Unit ☐	Individual ☐	Demo ☐	Meet/Greet ☐

Date: | Time of Day: | Location:

Training Objective:

# of Subjects / Hides:	Length/Size of Trail / Area:
Age of Trail/Hide(s):	# Turns/Transitions:
Scent Article: N/A ☐	Is It: Known ☐ Blind ☐ Dbl Blind ☐
Time on Trail / in Area:	Scent Specific? Yes ☐ No ☐ N/A ☐
DoT confirmed? Yes ☐ No ☐ N/A ☐	Field Tech: N/A ☐

Weather: N/A ☐	Temperature: Indoors ☐
Humidity: Low ☐ Medium ☐ High ☐	Wind Speed:	Direction:

Environment / Conditions:

Notes :

Reward:	Final Trained Response (FTR):

Mapping: North ⬆

Were objectives met?   Yes ☐   No ☐

Training Officer Review: ☐

K-9 TRAINING LOG

Unit ☐	Individual ☐	Demo ☐	Meet/Greet ☐
Date:	Time of Day:	Location:	

Training Objective:

_____

# of Subjects / Hides:	Length/Size of Trail / Area:
Age of Trail/Hide(s):	# Turns/Transitions:
Scent Article: N/A ☐	Is It: Known ☐ Blind ☐ Dbl Blind ☐
Time on Trail / in Area:	Scent Specific? Yes ☐ No ☐ N/A ☐
DoT confirmed? Yes ☐ No ☐ N/A ☐	Field Tech: N/A ☐

Weather: N/A ☐	Temperature: Indoors ☐
Humidity: Low ☐ Medium ☐ High ☐	Wind Speed:	Direction:

Environment / Conditions: _____

Notes : _____
_____
_____
_____
_____

Reward:	Final Trained Response (FTR):

Mapping: *North* ↑

Were objectives met?   Yes ☐   No ☐

Training Officer Review: ☐

K-9 TRAINING LOG

Unit ☐	Individual ☐	Demo ☐	Meet/Greet ☐
Date:	Time of Day:	Location:	

Training Objective:

_____

_____

# of Subjects / Hides:	Length/Size of Trail / Area:
Age of Trail/Hide(s):	# Turns/Transitions:
Scent Article: N/A ☐	Is It: Known ☐ Blind ☐ Dbl Blind ☐
Time on Trail / in Area:	Scent Specific? Yes ☐ No ☐ N/A ☐
DoT confirmed? Yes ☐ No ☐ N/A ☐	Field Tech: N/A ☐
Weather: N/A ☐	Temperature: Indoors ☐
Humidity: Low ☐ Medium ☐ High ☐	Wind Speed: Direction:

Environment / Conditions: _____

Notes : _____

_____

_____

_____

_____

Reward:	Final Trained Response (FTR):

Mapping: *North* ↑

Were objectives met?   Yes ☐   No ☐

Training Officer Review: ☐

K-9 TRAINING LOG

Unit ☐	Individual ☐	Demo ☐	Meet/Greet ☐

Date: | Time of Day: | Location:

Training Objective:

# of Subjects / Hides:	Length/Size of Trail / Area:
Age of Trail/Hide(s):	# Turns/Transitions:
Scent Article: N/A ☐	Is It: Known ☐ Blind ☐ Dbl Blind ☐
Time on Trail / in Area:	Scent Specific? Yes ☐ No ☐ N/A ☐
DoT confirmed? Yes ☐ No ☐ N/A ☐	Field Tech: N/A ☐

Weather: N/A ☐	Temperature: Indoors ☐
Humidity: Low ☐ Medium ☐ High ☐	Wind Speed:	Direction:

Environment / Conditions:

Notes :

Reward:	Final Trained Response (FTR):

Mapping: North ↑

Were objectives met?   Yes ☐   No ☐

Training Officer Review: ☐

K-9 TRAINING LOG

Unit ☐	Individual ☐	Demo ☐	Meet/Greet ☐
Date:	Time of Day:	Location:	

Training Objective:

# of Subjects / Hides:	Length/Size of Trail / Area:
Age of Trail/Hide(s):	# Turns/Transitions:
Scent Article: N/A ☐	Is It: Known ☐ Blind ☐ Dbl Blind ☐
Time on Trail / in Area:	Scent Specific? Yes ☐ No ☐ N/A ☐
DoT confirmed? Yes ☐ No ☐ N/A ☐	Field Tech: N/A ☐

Weather: N/A ☐	Temperature: Indoors ☐	
Humidity: Low ☐ Medium ☐ High ☐	Wind Speed:	Direction:

Environment / Conditions:

Notes :

Reward:	Final Trained Response (FTR):

Mapping: *North* ⬆

Were objectives met?   Yes ☐   No ☐

Training Officer Review: ☐

K-9 TRAINING LOG

Unit ☐	Individual ☐	Demo ☐	Meet/Greet ☐

Date: _____ Time of Day: _____ Location: _____

Training Objective: _____

_____

# of Subjects / Hides:	Length/Size of Trail / Area:
Age of Trail/Hide(s):	# Turns/Transitions:
Scent Article: N/A ☐	Is It: Known ☐ Blind ☐ Dbl Blind ☐
Time on Trail / in Area:	Scent Specific? Yes ☐ No ☐ N/A ☐
DoT confirmed? Yes ☐ No ☐ N/A ☐	Field Tech: N/A ☐
Weather: N/A ☐	Temperature: Indoors ☐
Humidity: Low ☐ Medium ☐ High ☐	Wind Speed: Direction:

Environment / Conditions: _____

_____

Notes : _____

_____

_____

_____

_____

Reward:	Final Trained Response (FTR):

Mapping: *North* ↑

Were objectives met? Yes ☐ No ☐

Training Officer Review: ☐

K-9 TRAINING LOG

Unit ☐	Individual ☐	Demo ☐	Meet/Greet ☐

Date:	Time of Day:	Location:

Training Objective:

# of Subjects / Hides:	Length/Size of Trail / Area:
Age of Trail/Hide(s):	# Turns/Transitions:
Scent Article: N/A ☐	Is It: Known ☐ Blind ☐ Dbl Blind ☐
Time on Trail / in Area:	Scent Specific? Yes ☐ No ☐ N/A ☐
DoT confirmed? Yes ☐ No ☐ N/A ☐	Field Tech: N/A ☐

Weather: N/A ☐	Temperature: Indoors ☐
Humidity: Low ☐ Medium ☐ High ☐	Wind Speed:	Direction:

Environment / Conditions:

Notes :

Reward:	Final Trained Response (FTR):

Mapping: North ↑

Were objectives met?   Yes ☐   No ☐

Training Officer Review: ☐

K-9 TRAINING LOG

Unit ☐	Individual ☐	Demo ☐	Meet/Greet ☐

Date:	Time of Day:	Location:

Training Objective:

# of Subjects / Hides:	Length/Size of Trail / Area:
Age of Trail/Hide(s):	# Turns/Transitions:
Scent Article: N/A ☐	Is It: Known ☐ Blind ☐ Dbl Blind ☐
Time on Trail / in Area:	Scent Specific? Yes ☐ No ☐ N/A ☐
DoT confirmed? Yes ☐ No ☐ N/A ☐	Field Tech: N/A ☐

Weather: N/A ☐	Temperature: Indoors ☐
Humidity: Low ☐ Medium ☐ High ☐	Wind Speed: Direction:

Environment / Conditions:

Notes :

Reward:	Final Trained Response (FTR):

Mapping: North ↑

Were objectives met?   Yes ☐   No ☐

Training Officer Review: ☐

K-9 TRAINING LOG

Unit ☐	Individual ☐	Demo ☐	Meet/Greet ☐
Date:	Time of Day:	Location:	

Training Objective:

# of Subjects / Hides:	Length/Size of Trail / Area:
Age of Trail/Hide(s):	# Turns/Transitions:
Scent Article: N/A ☐	Is It: Known ☐ Blind ☐ Dbl Blind ☐
Time on Trail / in Area:	Scent Specific? Yes ☐ No ☐ N/A ☐
DoT confirmed? Yes ☐ No ☐ N/A ☐	Field Tech: N/A ☐

Weather: N/A ☐	Temperature: Indoors ☐
Humidity: Low ☐ Medium ☐ High ☐	Wind Speed:	Direction:
Environment / Conditions:		

Notes :

Reward:	*Final Trained Response (FTR):*

Mapping: *North* ↑

Were objectives met?   Yes ☐   No ☐

Training Officer Review: ☐

K-9 TRAINING LOG

Unit ☐	Individual ☐	Demo ☐	Meet/Greet ☐

Date:	Time of Day:	Location:

Training Objective:

# of Subjects / Hides:	Length/Size of Trail / Area:
Age of Trail/Hide(s):	# Turns/Transitions:
Scent Article: N/A ☐	Is It: Known ☐ Blind ☐ Dbl Blind ☐
Time on Trail / in Area:	Scent Specific? Yes ☐ No ☐ N/A ☐
DoT confirmed? Yes ☐ No ☐ N/A ☐	Field Tech: N/A ☐

Weather: N/A ☐	Temperature: Indoors ☐
Humidity: Low ☐ Medium ☐ High ☐	Wind Speed: Direction:

Environment / Conditions:

Notes :

Reward:	Final Trained Response (FTR):

Mapping: *North* ⬆

Were objectives met?   Yes ☐   No ☐

Training Officer Review: ☐

K-9 TRAINING LOG

Unit ☐	Individual ☐	Demo ☐	Meet/Greet ☐
Date:	Time of Day:	Location:	

Training Objective:

# of Subjects / Hides:	Length/Size of Trail / Area:
Age of Trail/Hide(s):	# Turns/Transitions:
Scent Article: N/A ☐	Is It: Known ☐ Blind ☐ Dbl Blind ☐
Time on Trail / in Area:	Scent Specific? Yes ☐ No ☐ N/A ☐
DoT confirmed? Yes ☐ No ☐ N/A ☐	Field Tech: N/A ☐

Weather: N/A ☐	Temperature: Indoors ☐
Humidity: Low ☐ Medium ☐ High ☐	Wind Speed:	Direction:

Environment / Conditions:

Notes :

Reward:	Final Trained Response (FTR):

Mapping: North ⬆

Were objectives met?   Yes ☐   No ☐

Training Officer Review: ☐

K-9 TRAINING LOG

Unit ☐	Individual ☐	Demo ☐	Meet/Greet ☐

Date:	Time of Day:	Location:

Training Objective:

# of Subjects / Hides:	Length/Size of Trail / Area:
Age of Trail/Hide(s):	# Turns/Transitions:
Scent Article: N/A ☐	Is It: Known ☐ Blind ☐ Dbl Blind ☐
Time on Trail / in Area:	Scent Specific? Yes ☐ No ☐ N/A ☐
DoT confirmed? Yes ☐ No ☐ N/A ☐	Field Tech: N/A ☐

Weather: N/A ☐	Temperature: Indoors ☐
Humidity: Low ☐ Medium ☐ High ☐	Wind Speed:	Direction:

Environment / Conditions:

Notes :

Reward:	Final Trained Response (FTR):

Mapping: North ⬆

Were objectives met?   Yes ☐   No ☐

Training Officer Review: ☐

K-9 TRAINING LOG

Unit ☐	Individual ☐	Demo ☐	Meet/Greet ☐

Date:	Time of Day:	Location:

Training Objective:

_____

_____

# of Subjects / Hides:	Length/Size of Trail / Area:
Age of Trail/Hide(s):	# Turns/Transitions:
Scent Article: N/A ☐	Is It: Known ☐ Blind ☐ Dbl Blind ☐
Time on Trail / in Area:	Scent Specific? Yes ☐ No ☐ N/A ☐
DoT confirmed? Yes ☐ No ☐ N/A ☐	Field Tech: N/A ☐

Weather: N/A ☐	Temperature: Indoors ☐
Humidity: Low ☐ Medium ☐ High ☐	Wind Speed: Direction:

Environment / Conditions: _____

Notes : _____

_____

_____

_____

_____

Reward:	Final Trained Response (FTR):

Mapping: *North* ↑

Were objectives met?   Yes ☐   No ☐

Training Officer Review: ☐

K-9 TRAINING LOG

Unit ☐	Individual ☐	Demo ☐	Meet/Greet ☐

Date:	Time of Day:	Location:

Training Objective:

# of Subjects / Hides:	Length/Size of Trail / Area:
Age of Trail/Hide(s):	# Turns/Transitions:
Scent Article: N/A ☐	Is It: Known ☐ Blind ☐ Dbl Blind ☐
Time on Trail / in Area:	Scent Specific? Yes ☐ No ☐ N/A ☐
DoT confirmed? Yes ☐ No ☐ N/A ☐	Field Tech: N/A ☐

Weather: N/A ☐	Temperature: Indoors ☐
Humidity: Low ☐ Medium ☐ High ☐	Wind Speed: Direction:
Environment / Conditions:	

Notes :

Reward:	Final Trained Response (FTR):

Mapping: *North* ↑

Were objectives met? Yes ☐ No ☐

Training Officer Review: ☐

K-9 TRAINING LOG

Unit ☐	Individual ☐	Demo ☐	Meet/Greet ☐
Date:	Time of Day:	Location:	

Training Objective:

# of Subjects / Hides:	Length/Size of Trail / Area:
Age of Trail/Hide(s):	# Turns/Transitions:
Scent Article: N/A ☐	Is It: Known ☐ Blind ☐ Dbl Blind ☐
Time on Trail / in Area:	Scent Specific? Yes ☐ No ☐ N/A ☐
DoT confirmed? Yes ☐ No ☐ N/A ☐	Field Tech: N/A ☐
Weather: N/A ☐	Temperature: Indoors ☐
Humidity: Low ☐ Medium ☐ High ☐	Wind Speed: Direction:
Environment / Conditions:	

Notes :

Reward:	Final Trained Response (FTR):

Mapping: *North* ↑

Were objectives met?   Yes ☐   No ☐

Training Officer Review: ☐

K-9 TRAINING LOG

Unit ☐	Individual ☐	Demo ☐	Meet/Greet ☐

Date: Time of Day: Location:

Training Objective:

_____

_____

# of Subjects / Hides:	Length/Size of Trail / Area:
Age of Trail/Hide(s):	# Turns/Transitions:
Scent Article: N/A ☐	Is It: Known ☐ Blind ☐ Dbl Blind ☐
Time on Trail / in Area:	Scent Specific? Yes ☐ No ☐ N/A ☐
DoT confirmed? Yes ☐ No ☐ N/A ☐	Field Tech: N/A ☐

Weather: N/A ☐	Temperature: Indoors ☐
Humidity: Low ☐ Medium ☐ High ☐	Wind Speed: Direction:

Environment / Conditions:

_____

Notes :

_____

_____

_____

_____

_____

Reward:	Final Trained Response (FTR):

Mapping: *North* ↑

Were objectives met?   Yes ☐   No ☐

Training Officer Review: ☐

K-9 TRAINING LOG

Unit ☐	Individual ☐	Demo ☐	Meet/Greet ☐

| Date: | Time of Day: | Location: | |

Training Objective:

# of Subjects / Hides:	Length/Size of Trail / Area:
Age of Trail/Hide(s):	# Turns/Transitions:
Scent Article: N/A ☐	Is It: Known ☐ Blind ☐ Dbl Blind ☐
Time on Trail / in Area:	Scent Specific? Yes ☐ No ☐ N/A ☐
DoT confirmed? Yes ☐ No ☐ N/A ☐	Field Tech: N/A ☐

Weather: N/A ☐	Temperature: Indoors ☐
Humidity: Low ☐ Medium ☐ High ☐	Wind Speed:	Direction:

Environment / Conditions:

Notes :

Reward:	Final Trained Response (FTR):

Mapping: *North* ↑

Were objectives met?   Yes ☐   No ☐

Training Officer Review: ☐

K-9 TRAINING LOG

Unit ☐	Individual ☐	Demo ☐	Meet/Greet ☐

Date:	Time of Day:	Location:

Training Objective:

# of Subjects / Hides:	Length/Size of Trail / Area:
Age of Trail/Hide(s):	# Turns/Transitions:
Scent Article: N/A ☐	Is It: Known ☐ Blind ☐ Dbl Blind ☐
Time on Trail / in Area:	Scent Specific? Yes ☐ No ☐ N/A ☐
DoT confirmed? Yes ☐ No ☐ N/A ☐	Field Tech: N/A ☐

Weather: N/A ☐	Temperature: Indoors ☐
Humidity: Low ☐ Medium ☐ High ☐	Wind Speed: Direction:

Environment / Conditions:

Notes :

Reward:	Final Trained Response (FTR):

Mapping: *North* ⬆

Were objectives met?   Yes ☐   No ☐

Training Officer Review: ☐

K-9 TRAINING LOG

Unit ☐	Individual ☐	Demo ☐	Meet/Greet ☐

Date: | Time of Day: | Location:

Training Objective:

_____

_____

# of Subjects / Hides:	Length/Size of Trail / Area:
Age of Trail/Hide(s):	# Turns/Transitions:
Scent Article: N/A ☐	Is It: Known ☐ Blind ☐ Dbl Blind ☐
Time on Trail / in Area:	Scent Specific? Yes ☐ No ☐ N/A ☐
DoT confirmed? Yes ☐ No ☐ N/A ☐	Field Tech: N/A ☐

Weather: N/A ☐	Temperature: Indoors ☐
Humidity: Low ☐ Medium ☐ High ☐	Wind Speed:	Direction:

Environment / Conditions: _____

Notes :

_____

_____

_____

_____

Reward:	Final Trained Response (FTR):

Mapping: *North* ⬆

Were objectives met?   Yes ☐   No ☐

Training Officer Review: ☐

K-9 TRAINING LOG

Unit ☐	Individual ☐	Demo ☐	Meet/Greet ☐
Date:	Time of Day:	Location:	

Training Objective:

# of Subjects / Hides:	Length/Size of Trail / Area:
Age of Trail/Hide(s):	# Turns/Transitions:
Scent Article: N/A ☐	Is It: Known ☐ Blind ☐ Dbl Blind ☐
Time on Trail / in Area:	Scent Specific? Yes ☐ No ☐ N/A ☐
DoT confirmed? Yes ☐ No ☐ N/A ☐	Field Tech: N/A ☐

Weather: N/A ☐	Temperature: Indoors ☐
Humidity: Low ☐ Medium ☐ High ☐	Wind Speed: Direction:

Environment / Conditions:

Notes :

Reward:	Final Trained Response (FTR):

Mapping: *North* ↑

Were objectives met?   Yes ☐   No ☐

Training Officer Review: ☐

K-9 TRAINING LOG

Unit ☐	Individual ☐	Demo ☐	Meet/Greet ☐

Date:	Time of Day:	Location:

Training Objective:

# of Subjects / Hides:	Length/Size of Trail / Area:
Age of Trail/Hide(s):	# Turns/Transitions:
Scent Article: N/A ☐	Is It: Known ☐ Blind ☐ Dbl Blind ☐
Time on Trail / in Area:	Scent Specific? Yes ☐ No ☐ N/A ☐
DoT confirmed? Yes ☐ No ☐ N/A ☐	Field Tech: N/A ☐

Weather: N/A ☐	Temperature: Indoors ☐
Humidity: Low ☐ Medium ☐ High ☐	Wind Speed:	Direction:
Environment / Conditions:		

Notes :

Reward:	Final Trained Response (FTR):

Mapping: North ↑

Were objectives met?   Yes ☐   No ☐

Training Officer Review: ☐

K-9 TRAINING LOG

Unit ☐	Individual ☐	Demo ☐	Meet/Greet ☐

Date: _____ | Time of Day: _____ | Location: _____

Training Objective: _____

_____

_____

# of Subjects / Hides:	Length/Size of Trail / Area:
Age of Trail/Hide(s):	# Turns/Transitions:
Scent Article: N/A ☐	Is It: Known ☐ Blind ☐ Dbl Blind ☐
Time on Trail / in Area:	Scent Specific? Yes ☐ No ☐ N/A ☐
DoT confirmed? Yes ☐ No ☐ N/A ☐	Field Tech: N/A ☐

Weather: N/A ☐	Temperature: Indoors ☐
Humidity: Low ☐ Medium ☐ High ☐	Wind Speed:	Direction:

Environment / Conditions: _____

_____

Notes : _____

_____

_____

_____

_____

Reward:	*Final Trained Response (FTR):*

Mapping: *North* ↑

Were objectives met?   Yes ☐   No ☐

Training Officer Review: ☐

K-9 TRAINING LOG

Unit ☐	Individual ☐	Demo ☐	Meet/Greet ☐
Date:	Time of Day:	Location:	

Training Objective:

# of Subjects / Hides:	Length/Size of Trail / Area:
Age of Trail/Hide(s):	# Turns/Transitions:
Scent Article: N/A ☐	Is It: Known ☐ Blind ☐ Dbl Blind ☐
Time on Trail / in Area:	Scent Specific? Yes ☐ No ☐ N/A ☐
DoT confirmed? Yes ☐ No ☐ N/A ☐	Field Tech: N/A ☐

Weather: N/A ☐	Temperature: Indoors ☐
Humidity: Low ☐ Medium ☐ High ☐	Wind Speed: Direction:

Environment / Conditions:

Notes :

Reward:	Final Trained Response (FTR):

Mapping: *North* ↑

Were objectives met?   Yes ☐   No ☐

Training Officer Review: ☐

K-9 TRAINING LOG

Unit ☐	Individual ☐	Demo ☐	Meet/Greet ☐
Date:	Time of Day:	Location:	

Training Objective:

# of Subjects / Hides:	Length/Size of Trail / Area:
Age of Trail/Hide(s):	# Turns/Transitions:
Scent Article: N/A ☐	Is It: Known ☐ Blind ☐ Dbl Blind ☐
Time on Trail / in Area:	Scent Specific? Yes ☐ No ☐ N/A ☐
DoT confirmed? Yes ☐ No ☐ N/A ☐	Field Tech: N/A ☐

Weather: N/A ☐	Temperature:	Indoors ☐
Humidity: Low ☐ Medium ☐ High ☐	Wind Speed:	Direction:
Environment / Conditions:		

Notes :

Reward:	Final Trained Response (FTR):

Mapping: *North* ⬆

Were objectives met?   Yes ☐   No ☐

Training Officer Review: ☐

K-9 TRAINING LOG

Unit ☐	Individual ☐	Demo ☐	Meet/Greet ☐
Date:	Time of Day:	Location:	

Training Objective:

# of Subjects / Hides:	Length/Size of Trail / Area:
Age of Trail/Hide(s):	# Turns/Transitions:
Scent Article: N/A ☐	Is It: Known ☐ Blind ☐ Dbl Blind ☐
Time on Trail / in Area:	Scent Specific? Yes ☐ No ☐ N/A ☐
DoT confirmed? Yes ☐ No ☐ N/A ☐	Field Tech: N/A ☐

Weather: N/A ☐	Temperature: Indoors ☐	
Humidity: Low ☐ Medium ☐ High ☐	Wind Speed:	Direction:
Environment / Conditions:		

Notes :

Reward:	Final Trained Response (FTR):

Mapping: *North* ↑

Were objectives met?   Yes ☐   No ☐

Training Officer Review: ☐

K-9 TRAINING LOG

Unit ☐	Individual ☐	Demo ☐	Meet/Greet ☐

Date:	Time of Day:	Location:

Training Objective:

# of Subjects / Hides:	Length/Size of Trail / Area:
Age of Trail/Hide(s):	# Turns/Transitions:
Scent Article: N/A ☐	Is It: Known ☐ Blind ☐ Dbl Blind ☐
Time on Trail / in Area:	Scent Specific? Yes ☐ No ☐ N/A ☐
DoT confirmed? Yes ☐ No ☐ N/A ☐	Field Tech: N/A ☐

Weather: N/A ☐	Temperature: Indoors ☐
Humidity: Low ☐ Medium ☐ High ☐	Wind Speed: Direction:

Environment / Conditions:

Notes :

Reward:	Final Trained Response (FTR):

Mapping: *North* ↑

Were objectives met?   Yes ☐   No ☐

Training Officer Review: ☐

K-9 TRAINING LOG

Unit ☐	Individual ☐	Demo ☐	Meet/Greet ☐
Date:	Time of Day:	Location:	

Training Objective:

# of Subjects / Hides:	Length/Size of Trail / Area:
Age of Trail/Hide(s):	# Turns/Transitions:
Scent Article: N/A ☐	Is It: Known ☐ Blind ☐ Dbl Blind ☐
Time on Trail / in Area:	Scent Specific? Yes ☐ No ☐ N/A ☐
DoT confirmed? Yes ☐ No ☐ N/A ☐	Field Tech: N/A ☐
Weather: N/A ☐	Temperature: Indoors ☐
Humidity: Low ☐ Medium ☐ High ☐	Wind Speed:	Direction:

Environment / Conditions:

Notes :

Reward:	Final Trained Response (FTR):

Mapping: North ↑

Were objectives met?   Yes ☐ No ☐

Training Officer Review: ☐

K-9 TRAINING LOG

Unit ☐	Individual ☐	Demo ☐	Meet/Greet ☐

Date: | Time of Day: | Location:

Training Objective:

# of Subjects / Hides:	Length/Size of Trail / Area:
Age of Trail/Hide(s):	# Turns/Transitions:
Scent Article: N/A ☐	Is It: Known ☐ Blind ☐ Dbl Blind ☐
Time on Trail / in Area:	Scent Specific? Yes ☐ No ☐ N/A ☐
DoT confirmed? Yes ☐ No ☐ N/A ☐	Field Tech: N/A ☐

Weather: N/A ☐	Temperature: Indoors ☐
Humidity: Low ☐ Medium ☐ High ☐	Wind Speed:	Direction:

Environment / Conditions:

Notes :

Reward:	*Final Trained Response (FTR):*

Mapping: *North* ↑

Were objectives met?   Yes ☐   No ☐

Training Officer Review: ☐

K-9 TRAINING LOG

Unit ☐	Individual ☐	Demo ☐	Meet/Greet ☐
Date:	Time of Day:	Location:	

Training Objective:

# of Subjects / Hides:	Length/Size of Trail / Area:
Age of Trail/Hide(s):	# Turns/Transitions:
Scent Article: N/A ☐	Is It: Known ☐ Blind ☐ Dbl Blind ☐
Time on Trail / in Area:	Scent Specific? Yes ☐ No ☐ N/A ☐
DoT confirmed? Yes ☐ No ☐ N/A ☐	Field Tech: N/A ☐

Weather: N/A ☐	Temperature: Indoors ☐
Humidity: Low ☐ Medium ☐ High ☐	Wind Speed: Direction:

Environment / Conditions:

Notes :

Reward:	Final Trained Response (FTR):

Mapping: *North* ↑

Were objectives met?   Yes ☐   No ☐

Training Officer Review: ☐

K-9 TRAINING LOG

Unit ☐	Individual ☐	Demo ☐	Meet/Greet ☐

Date:	Time of Day:	Location:

Training Objective:

# of Subjects / Hides:	Length/Size of Trail / Area:
Age of Trail/Hide(s):	# Turns/Transitions:
Scent Article: N/A ☐	Is It: Known ☐ Blind ☐ Dbl Blind ☐
Time on Trail / in Area:	Scent Specific? Yes ☐ No ☐ N/A ☐
DoT confirmed? Yes ☐ No ☐ N/A ☐	Field Tech: N/A ☐

Weather: N/A ☐	Temperature: Indoors ☐
Humidity: Low ☐ Medium ☐ High ☐	Wind Speed: Direction:

Environment / Conditions:

Notes :

Reward:	Final Trained Response (FTR):

Mapping: *North* ⬆

Were objectives met?   Yes ☐   No ☐

Training Officer Review: ☐

K-9 TRAINING LOG

Unit ☐	Individual ☐	Demo ☐	Meet/Greet ☐

Date: | Time of Day: | Location:

Training Objective:
_____
_____
_____

# of Subjects / Hides:	Length/Size of Trail / Area:
Age of Trail/Hide(s):	# Turns/Transitions:
Scent Article: N/A ☐	Is It: Known ☐ Blind ☐ Dbl Blind ☐
Time on Trail / in Area:	Scent Specific? Yes ☐ No ☐ N/A ☐
DoT confirmed? Yes ☐ No ☐ N/A ☐	Field Tech: N/A ☐

Weather: N/A ☐	Temperature: Indoors ☐
Humidity: Low ☐ Medium ☐ High ☐	Wind Speed:	Direction:

Environment / Conditions: _____

Notes : _____
_____
_____
_____
_____

Reward:	Final Trained Response (FTR):

Mapping: North ⬆

Were objectives met?   Yes ☐   No ☐

Training Officer Review: ☐

K-9 TRAINING LOG

Unit ☐	Individual ☐	Demo ☐	Meet/Greet ☐

Date:	Time of Day:	Location:

Training Objective:

_____

# of Subjects / Hides:	Length/Size of Trail / Area:
Age of Trail/Hide(s):	# Turns/Transitions:
Scent Article: N/A ☐	Is It: Known ☐ Blind ☐ Dbl Blind ☐
Time on Trail / in Area:	Scent Specific? Yes ☐ No ☐ N/A ☐
DoT confirmed? Yes ☐ No ☐ N/A ☐	Field Tech: N/A ☐

Weather: N/A ☐	Temperature: Indoors ☐
Humidity: Low ☐ Medium ☐ High ☐	Wind Speed:	Direction:

Environment / Conditions: _____

Notes : _____

_____

_____

_____

Reward:	Final Trained Response (FTR):

Mapping: *North* ↑

Were objectives met?   Yes ☐ No ☐

Training Officer Review: ☐

K-9 TRAINING LOG

Unit ☐	Individual ☐	Demo ☐	Meet/Greet ☐

Date: _____ | Time of Day: _____ | Location: _____

Training Objective: _____

_____

# of Subjects / Hides:	Length/Size of Trail / Area:
Age of Trail/Hide(s):	# Turns/Transitions:
Scent Article: N/A ☐	Is It: Known ☐ Blind ☐ Dbl Blind ☐
Time on Trail / in Area:	Scent Specific? Yes ☐ No ☐ N/A ☐
DoT confirmed? Yes ☐ No ☐ N/A ☐	Field Tech: N/A ☐

Weather: N/A ☐	Temperature: Indoors ☐
Humidity: Low ☐ Medium ☐ High ☐	Wind Speed: Direction:

Environment / Conditions: _____

Notes : _____

_____

_____

_____

_____

Reward:	*Final Trained Response (FTR):*

Mapping: *North* ↑

Were objectives met?   Yes ☐   No ☐

Training Officer Review: ☐

K-9 TRAINING LOG

Unit ☐	Individual ☐	Demo ☐	Meet/Greet ☐

Date: _____ Time of Day: _____ Location: _____

Training Objective: _____

_____

_____

# of Subjects / Hides:	Length/Size of Trail / Area:
Age of Trail/Hide(s):	# Turns/Transitions:
Scent Article: N/A ☐	Is It: Known ☐ Blind ☐ Dbl Blind ☐
Time on Trail / in Area:	Scent Specific? Yes ☐ No ☐ N/A ☐
DoT confirmed? Yes ☐ No ☐ N/A ☐	Field Tech: N/A ☐

Weather: N/A ☐	Temperature: Indoors ☐
Humidity: Low ☐ Medium ☐ High ☐	Wind Speed: Direction:
Environment / Conditions:	

Notes : _____

_____

_____

_____

_____

Reward:	Final Trained Response (FTR):

Mapping: North ⬆

Were objectives met?   Yes ☐   No ☐

Training Officer Review: ☐

K-9 TRAINING LOG

Unit ☐	Individual ☐	Demo ☐	Meet/Greet ☐
Date:	Time of Day:	Location:	

Training Objective:

# of Subjects / Hides:	Length/Size of Trail / Area:
Age of Trail/Hide(s):	# Turns/Transitions:
Scent Article: N/A ☐	Is It: Known ☐ Blind ☐ Dbl Blind ☐
Time on Trail / in Area:	Scent Specific? Yes ☐ No ☐ N/A ☐
DoT confirmed? Yes ☐ No ☐ N/A ☐	Field Tech: N/A ☐

Weather: N/A ☐	Temperature: Indoors ☐
Humidity: Low ☐ Medium ☐ High ☐	Wind Speed: Direction:

Environment / Conditions:

Notes :

Reward:	Final Trained Response (FTR):

Mapping: *North* ⬆

Were objectives met? Yes ☐ No ☐

Training Officer Review: ☐

K-9 TRAINING LOG

Unit ☐	Individual ☐	Demo ☐	Meet/Greet ☐

Date:	Time of Day:	Location:

Training Objective:

# of Subjects / Hides:	Length/Size of Trail / Area:
Age of Trail/Hide(s):	# Turns/Transitions:
Scent Article: N/A ☐	Is It: Known ☐ Blind ☐ Dbl Blind ☐
Time on Trail / in Area:	Scent Specific? Yes ☐ No ☐ N/A ☐
DoT confirmed? Yes ☐ No ☐ N/A ☐	Field Tech: N/A ☐

Weather: N/A ☐	Temperature: Indoors ☐
Humidity: Low ☐ Medium ☐ High ☐	Wind Speed:	Direction:

Environment / Conditions:

Notes :

Reward:	Final Trained Response (FTR):

Mapping: North ↑

Were objectives met?   Yes ☐   No ☐

Training Officer Review: ☐

K-9 TRAINING LOG

Unit ☐	Individual ☐	Demo ☐	Meet/Greet ☐

Date:	Time of Day:	Location:

Training Objective: _____

_____

_____

# of Subjects / Hides:	Length/Size of Trail / Area:
Age of Trail/Hide(s):	# Turns/Transitions:
Scent Article: N/A ☐	Is It: Known ☐ Blind ☐ Dbl Blind ☐
Time on Trail / in Area:	Scent Specific? Yes ☐ No ☐ N/A ☐
DoT confirmed? Yes ☐ No ☐ N/A ☐	Field Tech: N/A ☐

Weather: N/A ☐	Temperature: Indoors ☐
Humidity: Low ☐ Medium ☐ High ☐	Wind Speed: Direction:

Environment / Conditions: _____

Notes : _____

_____

_____

_____

_____

Reward:	*Final Trained Response (FTR):*

Mapping: *North* ⬆

Were objectives met?   Yes ☐   No ☐

Training Officer Review: ☐

K-9 TRAINING LOG

Unit ☐	Individual ☐	Demo ☐	Meet/Greet ☐

Date:	Time of Day:	Location:

Training Objective:

# of Subjects / Hides:	Length/Size of Trail / Area:
Age of Trail/Hide(s):	# Turns/Transitions:
Scent Article: N/A ☐	Is It: Known ☐ Blind ☐ Dbl Blind ☐
Time on Trail / in Area:	Scent Specific? Yes ☐ No ☐ N/A ☐
DoT confirmed? Yes ☐ No ☐ N/A ☐	Field Tech: N/A ☐

Weather: N/A ☐	Temperature: Indoors ☐
Humidity: Low ☐ Medium ☐ High ☐	Wind Speed:	Direction:

Environment / Conditions:

Notes :

Reward:	Final Trained Response (FTR):

Mapping: North ↑

Were objectives met?   Yes ☐   No ☐

Training Officer Review: ☐

K-9 TRAINING LOG

Unit ☐	Individual ☐	Demo ☐	Meet/Greet ☐

Date:	Time of Day:	Location:

Training Objective:

_____

_____

# of Subjects / Hides:	Length/Size of Trail / Area:
Age of Trail/Hide(s):	# Turns/Transitions:
Scent Article: N/A ☐	Is It: Known ☐ Blind ☐ Dbl Blind ☐
Time on Trail / in Area:	Scent Specific? Yes ☐ No ☐ N/A ☐
DoT confirmed? Yes ☐ No ☐ N/A ☐	Field Tech: N/A ☐

Weather: N/A ☐	Temperature: Indoors ☐
Humidity: Low ☐ Medium ☐ High ☐	Wind Speed:	Direction:

Environment / Conditions: _____

Notes : _____

_____

_____

_____

_____

Reward:	*Final Trained Response (FTR):*

Mapping: *North* ↑

Were objectives met?   Yes ☐   No ☐

Training Officer Review: ☐

K-9 TRAINING LOG

Unit ☐	Individual ☐	Demo ☐	Meet/Greet ☐

Date:	Time of Day:	Location:

Training Objective:

# of Subjects / Hides:	Length/Size of Trail / Area:
Age of Trail/Hide(s):	# Turns/Transitions:
Scent Article: N/A ☐	Is It: Known ☐ Blind ☐ Dbl Blind ☐
Time on Trail / in Area:	Scent Specific? Yes ☐ No ☐ N/A ☐
DoT confirmed? Yes ☐ No ☐ N/A ☐	Field Tech: N/A ☐

Weather: N/A ☐	Temperature:	Indoors ☐
Humidity: Low ☐ Medium ☐ High ☐	Wind Speed:	Direction:

Environment / Conditions:

Notes :

Reward:	Final Trained Response (FTR):

Mapping: North ↑

Were objectives met?   Yes ☐   No ☐

Training Officer Review: ☐

K-9 TRAINING LOG

Unit ☐	Individual ☐	Demo ☐	Meet/Greet ☐
Date:	Time of Day:	Location:	

Training Objective:

# of Subjects / Hides:	Length/Size of Trail / Area:
Age of Trail/Hide(s):	# Turns/Transitions:
Scent Article: N/A ☐	Is It: Known ☐ Blind ☐ Dbl Blind ☐
Time on Trail / in Area:	Scent Specific? Yes ☐ No ☐ N/A ☐
DoT confirmed? Yes ☐ No ☐ N/A ☐	Field Tech: N/A ☐

Weather: N/A ☐	Temperature: Indoors ☐
Humidity: Low ☐ Medium ☐ High ☐	Wind Speed:	Direction:

Environment / Conditions:

Notes :

Reward:	Final Trained Response (FTR):

Mapping: North ⬆

Were objectives met?   Yes ☐   No ☐

Training Officer Review: ☐

K-9 TRAINING LOG

Unit ☐	Individual ☐	Demo ☐	Meet/Greet ☐
Date:	Time of Day:	Location:	

Training Objective:

# of Subjects / Hides:	Length/Size of Trail / Area:
Age of Trail/Hide(s):	# Turns/Transitions:
Scent Article: N/A ☐	Is It: Known ☐ Blind ☐ Dbl Blind ☐
Time on Trail / in Area:	Scent Specific? Yes ☐ No ☐ N/A ☐
DoT confirmed? Yes ☐ No ☐ N/A ☐	Field Tech: N/A ☐

Weather: N/A ☐	Temperature: Indoors ☐
Humidity: Low ☐ Medium ☐ High ☐	Wind Speed: Direction:
Environment / Conditions:	

Notes :

Reward:	Final Trained Response (FTR):

Mapping: North ↑

Were objectives met?   Yes ☐ No ☐

Training Officer Review: ☐

K-9 TRAINING LOG

Unit ☐	Individual ☐	Demo ☐	Meet/Greet ☐

Date: | Time of Day: | Location:

Training Objective:

# of Subjects / Hides:	Length/Size of Trail / Area:
Age of Trail/Hide(s):	# Turns/Transitions:
Scent Article: N/A ☐	Is It: Known ☐ Blind ☐ Dbl Blind ☐
Time on Trail / in Area:	Scent Specific? Yes ☐ No ☐ N/A ☐
DoT confirmed? Yes ☐ No ☐ N/A ☐	Field Tech: N/A ☐

Weather: N/A ☐	Temperature: Indoors ☐
Humidity: Low ☐ Medium ☐ High ☐	Wind Speed:	Direction:

Environment / Conditions:

Notes :

Reward: | Final Trained Response (FTR):

Mapping: North ⬆

Were objectives met?   Yes ☐   No ☐

Training Officer Review: ☐

K-9 TRAINING LOG

Unit ☐	Individual ☐	Demo ☐	Meet/Greet ☐

Date:	Time of Day:	Location:

Training Objective:

# of Subjects / Hides:	Length/Size of Trail / Area:
Age of Trail/Hide(s):	# Turns/Transitions:
Scent Article: N/A ☐	Is It: Known ☐ Blind ☐ Dbl Blind ☐
Time on Trail / in Area:	Scent Specific? Yes ☐ No ☐ N/A ☐
DoT confirmed? Yes ☐ No ☐ N/A ☐	Field Tech: N/A ☐

Weather: N/A ☐	Temperature: Indoors ☐
Humidity: Low ☐ Medium ☐ High ☐	Wind Speed:	Direction:

Environment / Conditions:

Notes :

Reward:	Final Trained Response (FTR):

Mapping: North ↑

Were objectives met?   Yes ☐   No ☐

Training Officer Review: ☐

K-9 TRAINING LOG

Unit ☐	Individual ☐	Demo ☐	Meet/Greet ☐

Date: Time of Day: Location:

Training Objective:

_____

_____

# of Subjects / Hides:	Length/Size of Trail / Area:
Age of Trail/Hide(s):	# Turns/Transitions:
Scent Article: N/A ☐	Is It: Known ☐ Blind ☐ Dbl Blind ☐
Time on Trail / in Area:	Scent Specific? Yes ☐ No ☐ N/A ☐
DoT confirmed? Yes ☐ No ☐ N/A ☐	Field Tech: N/A ☐

Weather: N/A ☐	Temperature: Indoors ☐
Humidity: Low ☐ Medium ☐ High ☐	Wind Speed: Direction:

Environment / Conditions: _____

Notes :

_____

_____

_____

_____

_____

Reward:	Final Trained Response (FTR):

Mapping: *North* ⬆

Were objectives met?   Yes ☐   No ☐

Training Officer Review: ☐

K-9 TRAINING LOG

Unit ☐	Individual ☐	Demo ☐	Meet/Greet ☐

Date:	Time of Day:	Location:

Training Objective: _____

_____

_____

# of Subjects / Hides:	Length/Size of Trail / Area:
Age of Trail/Hide(s):	# Turns/Transitions:
Scent Article: N/A ☐	Is It: Known ☐ Blind ☐ Dbl Blind ☐
Time on Trail / in Area:	Scent Specific? Yes ☐ No ☐ N/A ☐
DoT confirmed? Yes ☐ No ☐ N/A ☐	Field Tech: N/A ☐

Weather: N/A ☐	Temperature: Indoors ☐
Humidity: Low ☐ Medium ☐ High ☐	Wind Speed: Direction:

Environment / Conditions: _____

Notes : _____

_____

_____

_____

_____

Reward:	*Final Trained Response (FTR):*

Mapping: *North* ↑

Were objectives met?   Yes ☐   No ☐

Training Officer Review: ☐

K-9 TRAINING LOG

Unit ☐	Individual ☐	Demo ☐	Meet/Greet ☐
Date:	Time of Day:	Location:	

Training Objective:

# of Subjects / Hides:	Length/Size of Trail / Area:
Age of Trail/Hide(s):	# Turns/Transitions:
Scent Article: N/A ☐	Is It: Known ☐ Blind ☐ Dbl Blind ☐
Time on Trail / in Area:	Scent Specific? Yes ☐ No ☐ N/A ☐
DoT confirmed? Yes ☐ No ☐ N/A ☐	Field Tech: N/A ☐

Weather: N/A ☐	Temperature: Indoors ☐	
Humidity: Low ☐ Medium ☐ High ☐	Wind Speed:	Direction:

Environment / Conditions:

Notes :

Reward:	Final Trained Response (FTR):

Mapping: *North* ↑

Were objectives met?   Yes ☐   No ☐

Training Officer Review: ☐

K-9 TRAINING LOG

Unit ☐	Individual ☐	Demo ☐	Meet/Greet ☐

Date:	Time of Day:	Location:

Training Objective: _____

_____

# of Subjects / Hides:	Length/Size of Trail / Area:
Age of Trail/Hide(s):	# Turns/Transitions:
Scent Article: N/A ☐	Is It: Known ☐ Blind ☐ Dbl Blind ☐
Time on Trail / in Area:	Scent Specific? Yes ☐ No ☐ N/A ☐
DoT confirmed? Yes ☐ No ☐ N/A ☐	Field Tech: N/A ☐

Weather: N/A ☐	Temperature: Indoors ☐
Humidity: Low ☐ Medium ☐ High ☐	Wind Speed: Direction:

Environment / Conditions: _____

Notes : _____

_____

_____

_____

_____

Reward:	Final Trained Response (FTR):

Mapping: North ⬆

Were objectives met?   Yes ☐   No ☐

Training Officer Review: ☐

K-9 TRAINING LOG

Unit ☐	Individual ☐	Demo ☐	Meet/Greet ☐

Date:	Time of Day:	Location:

Training Objective:

# of Subjects / Hides:	Length/Size of Trail / Area:
Age of Trail/Hide(s):	# Turns/Transitions:
Scent Article: N/A ☐	Is It: Known ☐ Blind ☐ Dbl Blind ☐
Time on Trail / in Area:	Scent Specific? Yes ☐ No ☐ N/A ☐
DoT confirmed? Yes ☐ No ☐ N/A ☐	Field Tech: N/A ☐

Weather: N/A ☐	Temperature: Indoors ☐
Humidity: Low ☐ Medium ☐ High ☐	Wind Speed:	Direction:

Environment / Conditions:

Notes :

Reward:	Final Trained Response (FTR):

Mapping: _North ↑_

Were objectives met?   Yes ☐   No ☐

Training Officer Review: ☐

K-9 TRAINING LOG

Unit ☐	Individual ☐	Demo ☐	Meet/Greet ☐

Date:	Time of Day:	Location:

Training Objective:

# of Subjects / Hides:	Length/Size of Trail / Area:
Age of Trail/Hide(s):	# Turns/Transitions:
Scent Article: N/A ☐	Is It: Known ☐ Blind ☐ Dbl Blind ☐
Time on Trail / in Area:	Scent Specific? Yes ☐ No ☐ N/A ☐
DoT confirmed? Yes ☐ No ☐ N/A ☐	Field Tech: N/A ☐

Weather: N/A ☐	Temperature: Indoors ☐
Humidity: Low ☐ Medium ☐ High ☐	Wind Speed: Direction:

Environment / Conditions:

Notes :

Reward:	Final Trained Response (FTR):

Mapping: North ↑

Were objectives met?   Yes ☐   No ☐

Training Officer Review: ☐

K-9 TRAINING LOG

Unit ☐	Individual ☐	Demo ☐	Meet/Greet ☐

Date:	Time of Day:	Location:

Training Objective:

_____

_____

# of Subjects / Hides:	Length/Size of Trail / Area:
Age of Trail/Hide(s):	# Turns/Transitions:
Scent Article: N/A ☐	Is It: Known ☐ Blind ☐ Dbl Blind ☐
Time on Trail / in Area:	Scent Specific? Yes ☐ No ☐ N/A ☐
DoT confirmed? Yes ☐ No ☐ N/A ☐	Field Tech: N/A ☐

Weather: N/A ☐	Temperature: Indoors ☐
Humidity: Low ☐ Medium ☐ High ☐	Wind Speed:	Direction:
Environment / Conditions:		

Notes :

_____

_____

_____

_____

Reward:	Final Trained Response (FTR):

Mapping: North ↑

Were objectives met?   Yes ☐   No ☐

Training Officer Review: ☐

K-9 TRAINING LOG

Unit ☐	Individual ☐	Demo ☐	Meet/Greet ☐

Date:	Time of Day:	Location:

Training Objective:

_____

# of Subjects / Hides:	Length/Size of Trail / Area:
Age of Trail/Hide(s):	# Turns/Transitions:
Scent Article: N/A ☐	Is It: Known ☐ Blind ☐ Dbl Blind ☐
Time on Trail / in Area:	Scent Specific? Yes ☐ No ☐ N/A ☐
DoT confirmed? Yes ☐ No ☐ N/A ☐	Field Tech: N/A ☐

Weather: N/A ☐	Temperature: Indoors ☐
Humidity: Low ☐ Medium ☐ High ☐	Wind Speed:	Direction:

Environment / Conditions: _____

_____

Notes : _____

_____

_____

_____

_____

Reward:	Final Trained Response (FTR):

Mapping: North ⬆

Were objectives met?   Yes ☐   No ☐

Training Officer Review: ☐

K-9 TRAINING LOG

Unit ☐	Individual ☐	Demo ☐	Meet/Greet ☐

Date: | Time of Day: | Location:

Training Objective:

_____

_____

# of Subjects / Hides:	Length/Size of Trail / Area:
Age of Trail/Hide(s):	# Turns/Transitions:
Scent Article: N/A ☐	Is It: Known ☐ Blind ☐ Dbl Blind ☐
Time on Trail / in Area:	Scent Specific? Yes ☐ No ☐ N/A ☐
DoT confirmed? Yes ☐ No ☐ N/A ☐	Field Tech: N/A ☐

Weather: N/A ☐	Temperature: Indoors ☐
Humidity: Low ☐ Medium ☐ High ☐	Wind Speed:	Direction:

Environment / Conditions: _____

_____

Notes : _____

_____

_____

_____

_____

_____

Reward:	Final Trained Response (FTR):

Mapping: *North* ↑

Were objectives met?   Yes ☐   No ☐

Training Officer Review: ☐

K-9 TRAINING LOG

Unit ☐	Individual ☐	Demo ☐	Meet/Greet ☐

Date:	Time of Day:	Location:

Training Objective:

_____

_____

# of Subjects / Hides:	Length/Size of Trail / Area:
Age of Trail/Hide(s):	# Turns/Transitions:
Scent Article: N/A ☐	Is It: Known ☐ Blind ☐ Dbl Blind ☐
Time on Trail / in Area:	Scent Specific? Yes ☐ No ☐ N/A ☐
DoT confirmed? Yes ☐ No ☐ N/A ☐	Field Tech: N/A ☐

Weather: N/A ☐	Temperature: Indoors ☐
Humidity: Low ☐ Medium ☐ High ☐	Wind Speed:	Direction:

Environment / Conditions: _____

Notes : _____

_____

_____

_____

_____

Reward:	Final Trained Response (FTR):

Mapping: *North* ⬆

Were objectives met?   Yes ☐   No ☐

Training Officer Review: ☐

Glossary of Common Acronyms
(add your own in the spaces provided)

AS	Air Scent / Area Search
CoB	Change of Behaviors exhibited by the dog in odor
DoT	Direction of Travel of hider
FTR	Final Trained Response of dog upon finding target source (also known as alert or indication)
HRD	Human Remains Detection
LKP	Last Known Point of hider (starting point for trailing)
PLS	Point Last Seen of hider (starting point for trailing)
SS	Scent Specific (finding specific person among many)

About the Author

Sharolyn Sievert, an engineering coordinator by trade, has been active in search and rescue since 2003. She lives near Garfield, MN with her mother and her search dogs.

Author with K-9 Levia
Photo by The Wright Image

Sharolyn is an Air Force brat, her father having spent 20 years serving in the U.S. military. She was born on Mother's Day in Tachikawa, Japan. Her dad was an avid outdoorsman and hunter, however Sharolyn ended up going into hunting of a different type – using her K-9 partners to help find missing people.

Search and rescue gives her the ability to be outdoors, work with dogs and give something back to her community. Sharolyn over the years has trained and certified multiple search and rescue dogs in several different disciplines. She also has served as an instructor, an evaluator for K-9 teams, and maintains certification in a number of areas related to SAR beyond the K-9 work she loves.

Sharolyn is also a published author, and her books are available at:

www.K9SearchBooks.com

Printed in the United States of America.

Made in the USA
Las Vegas, NV
15 January 2023

65660419R00098